DATE DUE

DEMCO 128-5046

IRAQ

ABDO
Publishing Company

IRAQ

by Rebecca Rowell

Content Consultant
Babak Rahimi, Assistant Professor of Iranian and Islamic Studies
Program for the Study of Religion, Department of Literature, UC San Diego

CREDITS

Published by ABDO Publishing Company, 8000 West 78th Street, Edina, Minnesota 55439. Copyright © 2012 by Abdo Consulting Group, Inc. International copyrights reserved in all countries. No part of this book may be reproduced in any form without written permission from the publisher. The Essential Library™ is a trademark and logo of ABDO Publishing Company.

Printed in the United States of America,
North Mankato, Minnesota
062011
092011

MidAmerica bks 8-23-12 $24 95

Editor: Melissa Johnson
Copy Editor: Susan M. Freese
Design and production: Emily Love

About the Author: Rebecca Rowell has a Master of Arts in Publishing and Writing from Emerson College. She has edited numerous nonfiction children's books and written three biographies for younger readers.

Library of Congress Cataloging-in-Publication Data
Rowell, Rebecca.
 Iraq / by Rebecca Rowell.
    p. cm. -- (Countries of the world)
 Includes bibliographical references and index.
 ISBN 978-1-61783-113-3
 1. Iraq--Juvenile literature. I. Title.
 DS70.62.R69 2011
 956.7--dc23
                                          2011020920

Cover: Spiral minaret, Samarra, Iraq

TABLE OF CONTENTS

CHAPTER 1

A VISIT TO IRAQ

You walk down a busy sidewalk. Car horns blare. Impatient drivers are stuck in a traffic jam with carts and donkeys. You're nearing a busy souk, or street market. There, vendors are selling a variety of goods, including housewares, clothing, and food.

A man barters with a vendor over the price of a handwoven rug made of wool dyed maroon, mustard, black, and forest green. A few stalls away, a young woman admires silk scarves in rich jewel tones. Farther down, beans, spices, and fresh fruits are piled high in stalls in the food section of the souk. As you pass by, you're struck by the scent of cinnamon. An older couple fills a basket with figs and oranges. Some souks even offer services such as medical and dental care.

When shopping in a souk, it is common to bargain over prices.

This green-domed mosque rises over Baghdad.

SHOPPING AT NIGHT

Souks are busy during the day, but they are often even busier at night. The Middle East has a desert climate. During the summer, temperatures in much of Iraq near or exceed 100 degrees Fahrenheit (38°C). Because souks are outdoor markets, there is no escaping the heat while shopping in them. The only alternative is to stand in the shade, which provides little relief compared to the air conditioning found in an indoor shopping mall. Some relief comes after the setting of the sun. In the evening, the hot summer temperatures drop to an average of 80 degrees Fahrenheit (27°C).[1] Because of this, shopping at night is a popular activity.

The scene reminds you of the farmer's market at home. Vendors have been selling here for centuries, for as long as the city has been a center for trade.

Men, women, and children crowd the market. Some men are dressed in pants and shirts, while others wear traditional ankle-length, long-sleeved robes known as a *thawbs*. Many of the men are wearing turbans on their heads to protect them from the summer sun and heat. Women dress in a variety of clothing too. Some wear skirts and dresses that a Western woman might wear. Women in traditional attire wear abayas, cloaks that cover the wearers' clothing. Abayas are long, dark, and often plain, but some are more elaborate, embellished with gold thread and even fringes. The more ornate abayas are worn by wealthier women,

Souk vendors welcome shoppers to their stall.

BAGHDAD

In addition to being Iraq's capital, Baghdad is also the nation's largest city. And with approximately 5.8 million residents, the city is one of the most populous in the Middle East.[2] Baghdad was once called *Madinat al-Salam*, which is Arabic for "City of Peace."

Iraqi men and women generally do not touch in public.

some of whom also add a bejeweled belt to their outfits. A girl and her mother pass in front of you carrying bags of fruit and bread. Both are wearing head scarves.

It's the middle of the day, and the streets and sidewalks are alive with the activities of daily life. Even in summer temperatures that often approach 100 degrees Fahrenheit (38°C), the people conduct their affairs seemingly unaffected by the heat.

During your walk yesterday, the scene was darker—literally. A dust storm had blown across the city, creating hazy skies and covering everything with silt. Dust storms and sandstorms are common. Few people seemed fazed by the storms, though.

You are far from home and in a city very different from what you are accustomed to: Baghdad, Iraq. The abundance of sights and sounds in this city can be overwhelming. Yesterday, you saw the National Museum, home to ancient Iraqi treasures. It was damaged and looted in 2003 but restored and reopened to the public in 2009.

International boundary
Governorate boundary
⊛ National capital
◉ Governorate capital
• City or village

0 ——————— 50 Miles
0 ——————— 50 Kilometers

TURKEY

DAHUK
Dahuk ◉

Tigris *Great Zab*

ARBIL
Mosul ◉
◉ Arbil

NINAWA

Little Zab Al-Sulaymaniyyah ◉

SYRIA

Kirkuk ◉
KIRKUK
AL–SULAYMANIYYAH

SALAH AL–DIN
Tikrit ◉
Euphrates Samarra •
Khutaylah •

Lake Tharthar Al-Dujayl •

DIYALA
◉ Baqubah

Aqabah •
Al-Ramadi ◉ Fallujah • **Baghdad**
⊛ BAGHDAD

IRAQ

Ar Rutbah •

AL–ANBAR

Lake Milh *Tigris* WASIT

JORDAN

BABIL
Karbala ◉
KARBALA Al-Hillah ◉ ◉ Al-Kut

Al Kufah ◉ Al-Diwaniyah ◉
Al-Najaf ◉ AL–QADISIYYAH

Al-Amarah ◉
MAYSAN

AL–NAJAF

DHI QAR
Euphrates

Al-Samawah • Al-Nasiriyyah ◉

Shatt al-Arab

Basra ◉
BASRA
Al Faw •

SAUDI ARABIA

MUTHANNA

IRAN

Kuwait ◉
KUWAIT *Persian Gulf*

NORTH
↑

Political Boundaries of Iraq

Recent wars have greatly damaged Baghdad and the rest of Iraq.

Next, you make your way to the Tigris, the ancient river along which Baghdad was built. Often, the river is busy with fishermen hoping to catch dinner for their families. Perhaps the air will be a little cooler here, as the winds blow across the river's waters.

To your right, just past the market, stands a mosque. Its signature dome is adorned in intricate mosaics of gold and turquoise. Right now, this holy place is relatively quiet, but when a call to prayer is issued in a few hours, it will fill with people. Muslims are called to formal prayer five times each day. The *salat az-zuhr*, or noon prayer, had just finished before you headed out on your afternoon walk. The next prayer, *al-asr*, will be called in the late afternoon.

TRAVEL WARNING

The US Department of State warns US citizens against traveling in Iraq because of the ongoing violence and turmoil there. The government agency offers this explanation on its Web site: "Civilian air and road travel within Iraq remains dangerous. . . . Numerous insurgent groups remain active throughout Iraq. Although Iraqi Security Forces (ISF) operations against these groups continue, attacks against the ISF and US forces persist in many areas of the country. US citizens in Iraq remain at a high risk for kidnapping."[3]

A LAND OF CONTRASTS

You've been acquainting yourself with Baghdad for a week now. Before that, you visited Basra, located in the south near the Persian Gulf. You saw some of what remains of Iraq's marshlands, which have been lost almost completely. You've also been in northern Iraq, where the landscape is quite different again—hilly and green. Overall, the country is a land of contrasts. The landscape ranges from mountains to plains to deserts. Iraqis wear both traditional and Western clothing. And while many people around the world know of Iraq only because of the violence and upheaval here, the people of this young nation have a long history, reaching back to the origins of civilization.

During your trip, you've discovered that the turmoil, destruction, and devastation have not stifled the Iraqi spirit. Everywhere you've gone, the local people have treated you kindly. And on many of your walks, barefoot children playing in the streets have eagerly greeted you.

Exploring your surroundings and learning about the Iraqi people has been fascinating thus far. Now, as you walk through the city of Baghdad, you take in its sights, sounds, and smells. You can relate them to your own experiences. The men who sit for hours playing

In Iraq, men do not wear shorts and women do not wear sleeveless tops.

The Tigris River has shaped the region's history for thousands of years.

backgammon outside cafés remind you of playing checkers with your grandfather when you were a child.

As you wander Baghdad's ancient streets, you wonder how Iraq will recover from its recent history. The United States fought Iraq in 1991 during the Gulf War and then invaded in 2003 to begin what is now known as the war in Iraq. The war and violence have brought Iraq to the world's attention, often on a daily basis. But Iraq is more than a Middle Eastern nation trying to recover from crisis. It's a land unlike any other, with a history, culture, traditions, landscape, and people all its own. And you look forward to learning all about it.

SNAPSHOT

Official name: Republic of Iraq (Arabic: Jumhuriyat al-Iraq)

Capital city: Baghdad

Form of government: parliamentary democracy

Title of leader: president

Currency: Iraqi dinar

Population (July 2011 est.): 30,399,572
World rank: 39

Size: 169,236 square miles (438,317 sq km)
World rank: 58

Language: Arabic and Kurdish

Official religion: Islam

Per capita GDP (2010, US dollars): $3,600
World rank: 160

CHAPTER 2

GEOGRAPHY: MORE THAN DESERT

Iraq is located in the eastern part of the Middle East, an area that includes southwest Asia and parts of northern Africa. The country has an area of 169,235 square miles (438,317 sq km), which makes it about twice the size of Idaho. Almost all of this area—168,868 square miles (437,367 sq km)—is land.[1] The remainder is water.

Iraq shares borders with six other nations. Going clockwise from Iraq's eastern border, the nations are Iran, Kuwait, Saudi Arabia, Jordan, Syria, and Turkey. Iraq's longest border is with Iran.

Similar to other countries in the Middle East, Iraq is known for its hot, dry deserts. But Iraq offers more than an arid landscape, and the country also

The area between the Tigris and Euphrates Rivers is often called "the cradle of civilization."

Northeastern Iraq is mountainous.

has marshes, plains, and mountains. Iraq is almost landlocked. A very small portion of the country—12 miles (19 km) between the borders with Iran and Kuwait—is coastline on the northern Persian Gulf.[2]

THE SHAPE OF THE LAND

Iraq has four distinct regions: desert; alluvial plains, or lower valley; Al-Jazirah, an arid plateau area; and highlands, a mountainous region. Each area has its own distinct landscape and climate.

The desert landscape occupies Iraq's western and southern areas. The country has approximately 65,000 square miles (168,000 sq km) of desert, covering almost 40 percent of its total area.[3] The desert in the west is part of the Syrian Desert, which continues into Syria and Jordan. The desert in the south is known by two names: Al-Dibdibah in the southeast and Al-Hajarah in the northwest. Whereas Al-Dibdibah

TURKEY

Cropland
Pasture
Wetland
Desert

International boundary
⊛ National capital
• City

0　　　50 Miles
0　　　50 Kilometers

Taurus Mountains

• Dahuk

Tigris

Great Zab

Ghundah Zhur

Mosul •

Sinjar Mountains

• Arbil

SYRIA

Al-Jazirah

Little Zab

• Al-Sulaymaniyyah

Kirkuk •

Zagros Mountains

Euphrates

Uzaym

Khutaylah •

Tikrit •

Samarra •

Diyala

Lake Tharthar

Al-Dujayl •

IRAN

Aqabah •
Al-Ramadi •

Fallujah •

• Baqubah

⊛ **Baghdad**

Ar Rutbah •

IRAQ

Mesopotamia

Tigris

JORDAN

Syrian Desert

Lake Milh

Karbala •

• Al-Kut

Al-Hillah •

Al Kufah •
Al-Najaf •

• Al-Diwaniyah

• Al-Amarah

Euphrates

Shatt al-Arab

Al-Samawah •

Al-Hajarah

Al-Nasiriyyah •

Lake Hammar Basra •

SAUDI ARABIA

Al Faw •

Al-Dibdibah

KUWAIT ⊛ Kuwait

Persian Gulf

NORTH
↑

Geography of Iraq

is sandy and has scrub vegetation, Al-Hajarah is rocky with ridges, depressions, and wadis, or river valleys that are dry for much of the year.

Another significant portion of Iraq—nearly one-third of the country—consists of alluvial plains. Also known as floodplains, the alluvial plains are flat lands next to rivers and streams. More than 51,000 square miles (132,000 sq km) of central and southeastern Iraq are covered by plains.[5] The water comes from the Tigris and Euphrates Rivers, which merge in southeastern Iraq to become the Shatt al-Arab, a river that flows 120 miles (193 km) before emptying into the Persian Gulf.[6] This area has a low elevation and poor drainage. As a result, it floods seasonally.

These areas have marshlands and lakes as well. In the summer, some of the marshlands dry up. Hawr al-Hammar, or Lake Hammar, is

WADIS

The word *wadi* comes from the similar Arabic word *wādi* and is used to identify a dry riverbed that floods when it rains. This kind of typography is often referred to as a gully or a wash in the United States. The term also describes a sharp depression or indentation in the desert. The Middle East has several wadis. In Iraq, Al-Batin is an important wadi. This 45-mile (72-km) stretch of land in the southern part of the country has served as the border between Iraq and Kuwait since the early twentieth century.[7]

The Shatt al-Arab forms a part of Iraq's border with Iran.

an extensive swampy lake, measuring 750 square miles (1,950 sq km) and stretching 70 miles (110 km) east to west.[8]

Northern Iraq presents a third topographical region, known as Al-Jazirah. Arabic for "the Island," the region's name denotes its location. Al-Jazirah is north of the alluvial plains, in the area between the Tigris and Euphrates Rivers—an area that extends into Syria. This arid section of the country is a plateau. The Sinjar Mountains are located here, as are several *sabkhahs*, or salt flats, the largest of which is Milhat Ashqar.

The fourth and final region is in northeast Iraq. There, the highlands area has a varied landscape of plains, hills, and mountains that covers approximately 20 percent of the nation. One-quarter of this area is mountainous and includes the Taurus and Zagros Mountains. Iraq's highest point, Ghundah Zhur, is 11,834 feet (3,607 m) tall and located on the border with Iran.[9] Mountains continue along Iraq's border with Turkey. The highest mountains have the only forests in Iraq.

Several tributaries of the Tigris flow through this area, including the Great Zab, Little Zab, Diyala, and Uzaym Rivers. The many rivers and streams have cut through the mountains over time, leaving some deep gorges, including Ru Kuchuk and Bekma.

CLIMATE

Iraq's climate varies with its topography. The lower-level lands of the plains and deserts are hot and dry. These regions experience two seasons—summer and winter—which are separated by a short period of transition. Summer occurs from May to October and is filled with sunny, extremely hot days. There is no rainfall from June through September. During the other months, between November and April, the lowlands receive precipitation, but it is less than ten inches (25 cm) per year.[10] Winter spans from December to February and brings cooler weather, though it is never cold in Iraq.

The climate of the northeast is opposite that of the lowlands in terms of season length. Summer is short, and winter is long. Northeast summers are hot and dry, with temperatures approximately five to ten degrees Fahrenheit (3 to 6°C) lower than lowland temperatures.[11]

Irrigation is necessary to grow anything in Iraq's desert lowland regions.

AVERAGE TEMPERATURES AND RAINFALL

Region (City)	Average January Temperature Minimum/ Maximum	Average July Temperature Minimum/Maximum	Average Rainfall January/July
Central (Baghdad)	39/61°F (4/16°C)	75/109°F (24/43°C)	0.91/0 inches (2.3/0 cm)
South (Basra)	45/64°F (7/18°C)	81/104°F (27/40°C)	1.42/0 inches (3.6/0 cm)
Northern Plains (Mosul)	36/54°F (2/12°C)	79/106°F (26/41°C)	1.61/0 inches (4.1/0 cm)[13]

The northeast receives more precipitation than the lowlands. The foothills there average 12 to 22 inches (30 to 56 cm) per year. The mountains receive considerably more precipitation—sometimes, more than 40 inches (102 cm), much of which comes in the form of snow.[12] As in the lowlands, precipitation in the highlands comes during the winter months, and little rain falls during the summer. Sometimes, the melting winter snows cause flooding in central and southern Iraq.

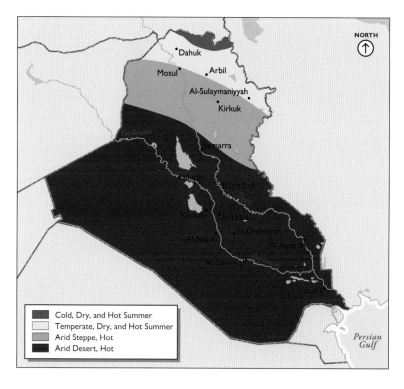

■	Cold, Dry, and Hot Summer
□	Temperate, Dry, and Hot Summer
▨	Arid Steppe, Hot
■	Arid Desert, Hot

Climate of Iraq

The entire nation is affected by the *shamal*, a summer wind that blows steadily from the north and northwest into Iraq and Iran and across the Arabian Peninsula. During the summer, the shamal is almost constant. It brings very dry air that prevents cloud formation and leads to high temperatures. Another wind, called the *sharqi*, is the opposite of the shamal. It blows from the south and southeast during the early summer and early winter.

Both types of winds cause dust storms. Such storms take place in Iraq most of the year but are especially frequent during June and July.

The word *shamal* comes from the Arabic *samal,* meaning "north."

Seasonal winds bring sandstorms to Iraq.

CHAPTER 3

ANIMALS AND NATURE: ADAPTED TO THE LAND

The deserts, plains, and mountains of Iraq all have species that represent their respective landscapes and climates. Antelope, cheetahs, gazelles, and hyenas live in Iraqi deserts. Camel spiders, scorpions, snakes, and lizards also live in the deserts.

Other varieties of animals make Iraq's mountains their home. Wolves, foxes, and cheetahs are the largest animals in this habitat. Smaller animals include badgers, muskrats, otters, and porcupines. A variety of insects, such as spiders and locusts, live in the mountains as well.

Iraq's rivers and lakes have abundant fish, including carp, catfish, and loach. Dozens of species of birds wing across the country's skies. These include herons, ducks,

Lions once lived in Iraq, but they are now extinct in the country.

The diadem rat snake is one of Iraq's many desert snake species.

ENDANGERED SPECIES IN IRAQ

According to the International Union for Conservation of Nature (IUCN), Iraq is home to the following numbers of species that are categorized by the organization as Critically Endangered, Endangered, or Vulnerable:

Mammals	13
Birds	18
Reptiles	2
Amphibians	1
Fishes	11
Mollusks	0
Other Invertebrates	15
Plants	0
Total	60[1]

and partridges, which are native to the watery marshlands. Other areas are home to owls, eagles, hawks, and sparrows. Buzzards and vultures are common in the desert.

VEGETATION

Iraq's desert landscape is sparse in vegetation but includes tamarisk and milfoil, or yarrow. Tamarisk is the general name given to a collection of shrubs and trees common in the desert. The tamarisk found in Iraq is also known as the eshel, athel tree, leafless tamarisk, and salt cedar. It is an evergreen that grows quickly and reaches up

The steppe eagle's range extends across Asia.

to 59 feet (18 m) in height. Its leaves are wiry, scaly, and bluish-green, although some twigs are bare. When the tamarisk shrub blooms, it produces an abundance of tiny pink flowers.

Yarrow, like tamarisk, is a category that includes numerous plants—in this case, more than 100 species of a perennial herb, a plant that grows year after year without replanting. The flowers are yellow and tend to grow in groups that form a flat top. Yarrow is used to make tea in some cultures.

One Iraqi species of tamarisk, *Tamarix ramosissima*, is found across Asia from Iraq to China.

The areas of Iraq that are cooler and wetter than the desert are more hospitable to plants and thus have more vegetation. The most fertile land lies along the Tigris and Euphrates Rivers, where water is abundant. There, trees and plants flourish, including willows, poplars, alders, licorice, and bulrushes. Other wet areas—the lakes and marshlands—are havens for plants such as reeds, geranium flowers, and pimpernel, a type of herb. The date palm is common in Iraq, particularly in the south. Dozens of varieties of this tree dot the landscape.

Northwestern Iraq is a steppe region, which is free of trees but home to many herbs and shrubs, including thyme, goosefoot, and mugwort. Many grasses thrive in this region as well. Finally, the mountains are home to many types of trees. The lower slopes are populated with

Date palm trees are common in the wetter areas of Iraq.

AL-MISHRAQ SULFUR FIRE

In 2003, Iraq suffered a major environmental disaster when a fire broke out in Mosul at Al-Mishraq, a sulfur plant. Sulfur is used in industry to develop products from paper to insecticides. Most sulfur is converted to sulfuric acid and used to manufacture a variety of items, including fertilizers, pigments, detergents, and sheet metal.

The Al-Mishraq fire was started by arsonists on June 24 and burned for one month. Hundreds of thousands of tons of sulfur burned, producing sulfur dioxide gas. This gas is corrosive and toxic, and once it is in the atmosphere, it can combine with water and fall back to the earth as acid rain.

The sulfur cloud from the fire caused respiratory problems for many people and at least two deaths. In addition, acid rain destroyed wheat crops or stunted the plants' growth. Damage to these crops affected the nation's food supply and commerce. The disaster was estimated to have caused US$40 million in damage to crops in the area.[2] The long-term effects are not known, although researchers believe the environmental impact will not be long lasting.

hawthorns, junipers, wild pears, and terebinths—small trees that are part of the cashew family.

ENVIRONMENTAL THREATS

Although many plants and animals are thriving in Iraq today, others are threatened by the actions of humans. For example, water projects have damaged Iraq's marshlands. Dams were built to control flooding. During the 1970s and 1980s, the Tigris and Euphrates Rivers were connected with canals to help bring water to dry areas during times of drought. However, these structures blocked and diverted water from the marshlands.

A second large canal project was completed in the 1990s, the stated goal of which was to improve irrigation and drainage in agricultural areas. But evidence indicates that this project also drained large areas of marshlands in the south and that this drainage was not an accident. Rather, it was in response to rebel attacks that had occurred in the area against government forces—something that has been common in Iraq's long, tumultuous history. The government drained the marshlands to punish these forces, which relied on the water for survival, and to destroy their hiding places.

Iraq's various dams and canals have destroyed approximately 90 percent of the marshlands in southern Iraq.[3] As a result, much of the area has been transformed into dry salt flats, negatively affecting the wildlife and vegetation in the area.

Additional threats to Iraq's environment and people have come from abandoned factories, military scrap yards, and battle sites. These sites

THE MADAN

The changes caused by the loss of Iraq's southern marshlands affected more than the wildlife in the area. The Madan people lived in the area and relied on the plants and wildlife supported by the marshlands. These people lived off the land, eating products of the marshes, such as rice, fish, and edible rushes, which they also used for building homes and boats. The draining of the marshlands destroyed the Madans' way of life, and many were forced to move.

Conservation groups are working to protect
Iraq's wetlands and the people who live there.

poison the areas around them with toxic substances such as sulfur,
cyanide, and uranium. The hazardous materials found in many locations
in Iraq can seep into the ground and poison the groundwater, harming
animals and people.

Considerable work is needed to address the environmental issues in Iraq. Without conservation efforts, the nation's remaining marshlands will be lost. Even greater efforts are needed to restore the existing marshlands. Several areas have been set aside to protect Iraq's valuable marshlands, including the Mesopotamia Marshlands National Park, the Hor Al-Hammar Marshes Protected Area, the Wadi Tharthar Lake and Marshes Protected Area, the Hawizeh Marshes Wetlands, Hor Suweicha Wetland Protected Area, Nasiriya Marshes Protected Area, Habbaniya Lake Protected Area, and Shatra Marshes Protected Area. An organization called Nature Iraq is striving, with some success, to save the marshlands and other areas of Iraq, along with the animals that live there.

IRAQ'S NATURE

Nature Iraq is a nongovernmental organization focused on maintaining and restoring Iraq's environment and wildlife. The organization works with the United Nations Environment Programme (UNEP) and is affiliated with Birdlife International. According to Nature Iraq, its members "work to protect, restore, and preserve Iraq's natural environment and the rich cultural heritage it nourishes."[4]

The organization's members are a varied group that includes scientists, environmentalists, photographers, administrators, and translators. In addition to preserving and recovering Iraq's flora and fauna, Nature Iraq also gathers information to better understand the state of the nation's varied regions and wildlife.

CHAPTER 4

HISTORY: NEW CIVILIZATIONS TO A NEW BEGINNING

Iraq's history goes back thousands of years to the beginning of civilization. Iraq occupies land that was once known as Mesopotamia, located between the Tigris and Euphrates Rivers. The word *Mesopotamia* is Greek for "land between the rivers." This fertile land provided an excellent location for people to settle. The Sumerians, who came from Iran and northern Anatolia, came to the region around 3500 BCE.

MANY KINGDOMS, MANY RULERS

The Sumer kingdom controlled the area for more than 1,000 years. Under Sumerian rule, many changes occurred in Mesopotamia. Farming

Babylonian lion statue

improved, canals were introduced, and architecture and building both advanced. The Sumerians had several major communities—city-states ruled by kings that focused on culture, the economy, and politics. Great thinkers invented both the cuneiform writing system and mathematics. The Sumerian culture spread beyond the city-states to the Middle East, influencing other cultures.

Around 2350 BCE, the Sumerians joined with another group, the Akkadians. The Sumer and Akkad kingdoms became a single nation ruled by King Sargon of Akkad. A few centuries later, in 2000 BCE, control shifted when the Amorites came to power. During the Amorites' rule, the city of Babylon became a center of politics and commerce, and Babylonia became a great empire.

Babylonia's sixth and best-known ruler was

PREHISTORIC IRAQ

The Sumerians were not the first people to live in Mesopotamia. The region's long history extends well beyond the Sumerian era, and Iraq's prehistory goes back thousands of years.

In approximately 60,000 BCE, a Neanderthal man was buried in the Shanidar cave, located in the Zagros Mountains in Kurdistan. Excavation of this site between 1953 and 1960 revealed not only human bones but also evidence that sheep and goats were domesticated there for food around 9000 BCE—the earliest evidence of animals domesticated for food ever discovered.

Around 7000 BCE, Jarmo was settled in northeastern Iraq, near present-day Kirkuk. Excavation of this site has provided important evidence of what is believed to be one of the first farming settlements, including domesticated grains and animals. Archaeologists have also unearthed sickle blades, stones for milling, and pottery.

Hammurabi (reigned 1792–1750 BCE). When Hammurabi ascended to power, he united the multiple city-states of Mesopotamia. In addition, he was the first person to write down a set of laws. The Code of Hammurabi set down 282 laws that addressed economic provisions, family law, and criminal law.

Baked clay tablet with cuneiform text

Babylonia began declining following Hammurabi's death. Then, in 1595 BCE, another group took control of the area: the Kassites. Their empire lasted four centuries, although it did not regain the greatness achieved under Hammurabi. Assyria, a section of the empire, broke away in the thirteenth century BCE to form its own empire and challenged the Kassite Empire. In 1158 BCE, the Elamites, a neighboring society, conquered the Kassites.

Kings came and went, each fighting to control his holdings in Mesopotamia. Eventually, Babylonia was seized by Persia (now Iran) and lost its independence. Persia became a mighty power in the sixth century BCE. It was overthrown in the early fourth century, however, by Alexander III of Macedon (356–323 BCE), a warrior who conquered the area for the Greeks. Known as Alexander the Great, he took control of Babylonia in 331 BCE. He intended to make the great city of Babylon the capital of his empire, but he died before achieving his goal.

Seleucus I, one of Alexander's generals, took over, beginning the Greek Seleucid kingdom in Babylon in 312 BCE. The Persians recaptured the area 200 years later, in the mid-second century BCE. This time, their rule continued for several hundred years, until a new group of invaders arrived.

ANCIENT ACHIEVEMENTS

Many achievements by Iraq's earliest peoples continue to be part of everyday modern life. For example, the Sumerians developed irrigation systems, cereal agriculture, and the seed plow. They also developed cuneiform, the oldest known form of writing, and invented the potter's wheel and the sailboat. The Sumerians were talented writers, musicians, and architects, as well.

In addition, the Babylonians influenced math and astronomy with their sexagesimal system, which is based on the number 60. One example is time: an hour is divided into 60 minutes, and one minute equals 60 seconds. Babylon is also known for its hanging gardens, built by Nebuchadnezzar II (reigned 605–562 BCE). The Hanging Gardens of Babylon were one of the seven wonders of the ancient world.

THE INTRODUCTION OF ISLAM

The Prophet Muhammad (570–632 CE) founded the religion of Islam in the Arabian Peninsula (now Saudi Arabia). In the years immediately after his death, his followers left Arabia to spread the new religion. In 637, these Muslim Arabs defeated Persia. The land that would become Iraq became a caliphate. In 750, the Arabic Abbasid dynasty—named for al-Abbas, Muhammad's uncle—was established in Iraq.

The dynasty ruled more than 500 years, and during this time, the cultures of Persia and the Muslim Arabs merged. The Abbasids developed

MUSLIMS DIVIDED: SUNNIS AND SHIITES

Followers of Islam are known as Muslims, and they affiliate with one of two groups: Sunni or Shiite (also called Shia). The word *Sunni* comes from the Arabic *sunna*, which means "tradition." The word *Shiite* or *Shia* comes from the Arabic *shia,* which means "partisan." While the two groups agree on the central principles of Islam, they disagree about who are the rightful successors to Muhammad, the founder of Islam. Specifically, Sunnis and Shiites disagree about the place of Ali, who was Muhammad's cousin and son-in-law.

Muslims split into these two groups not long after Muhammad's death in 632. Abu Bakr became Muhammad's caliph, or successor. He was followed by Umar I and Uthman. Uthman was murdered in 656, and Ali became the next leader.

Mu'awiya was Uthman's cousin and the governor of Damascus. He would not recognize Ali as caliph until Uthman's killers were found. Ali ended the dispute with a compromise, but this weakened his position as supreme leader. Ali died in 661 when one of his own followers killed him.

Sunnis consider Ali the fourth and final caliph. Shiites believe Ali should have been the first caliph and that his successors should have been Ali's direct descendents.

a mighty empire in which the arts, commerce, industry, and science flourished. The Abbasids expanded the caliphate, heading east for the first time, and Baghdad became the capital.

Caliph is short for khalifah rasul Allah, or "successor of the Messenger of God."

The empire's power eventually reached its limits, however, and it began declining when non-Muslim forces were allowed into the caliph's personal army. This change led to a loss of unity within the army. The dynasty weakened, and parts of the empire devolved to local control. The Seljuqs, a Turkish tribe, conquered Baghdad in 1055. The Seljuqs took political control but allowed the Abbasid caliph to maintain his religious power. The Abbasid dynasty ultimately ended in 1258 when the Mongols conquered Baghdad. Under the Mongols, Iraq was divided into small kingdoms.

OTTOMAN AND BRITISH RULE

Iraq remained divided for 300 years. Then, in 1534, the Ottomans, a Turkish group, took over Baghdad. These people came from the Ottoman Empire, which included present-day Turkey, Egypt, Syria, Greece, and parts of the Balkans and Saudi Arabia, including Mecca, the birthplace of Muhammad and Islam's holiest city.

The spiral minaret in Samarra was built by the Abbasid caliphs.

Ottoman rule continued for almost 400 years. Then, in the early twentieth century, many of the Arabs under Ottoman rule wanted their own countries, free of Turkish control. Also during this time, nations in Europe and elsewhere fought in World War I (1914–1918). When the Ottomans allied with the Germans during the war, the Arabs thought they had the opportunity to obtain their freedom.

Groups of Arabs revolted against the Ottoman Empire. The British were fighting against the Germans and the Turks and therefore supported the Arab uprisings. The British wanted to create opportunities in the Middle East for the Anglo-Persian Oil Company, so they sent troops to challenge the Turks in Al-Kut in 1914. The British were defeated and surrendered in April 1916, but the government sent more troops. The British took over Baghdad the following March.

After World War I ended in 1918, the League of Nations, a multinational organization, mandated that the region of Iraq be placed under control of the United Kingdom. Many Iraqis were not happy under British control, and some groups rebelled. In the north, the Kurds wanted their own country. In response, the United Kingdom established a monarchy in Iraq, uniting several different tribes and ethnic groups into one nation. Faisal I, an Iraqi, was made king in 1921. However, the British continued supervising the Iraqi government.

King Faisal I, 1932

In addition, the United Kingdom and Iraq signed a treaty of alliance and drafted a constitution for Iraq. The constitution, known as the Organic Law, was adopted in 1924 and set forth a constitutional monarchy. Iraq was to have a monarch, Faisal, who shared power with a parliamentary government of two houses. This bicameral legislature consisted of a House of Representatives with elected officials and a Senate with appointed officials. The constitution went into effect the following year, after Faisal signed it on March 21, 1925.

Faisal I was from Mecca (in modern Saudi Arabia) and was king of Syria from 1918 to 1920.

The British gave up the last of their control in 1932. Faisal I died in 1933. He had two successors, although the United Kingdom took over Iraq during World War II (1939–1945). When the war ended, Iraq became a founding member of two organizations: the United Nations (UN) and the Arab League. Iraq seemed to be on a positive track, moving forward as an independent nation. But in 1958, the monarchy ended with a violent coup. Iraq was declared a republic, no longer under the rule of a monarch.

TEN YEARS OF UNREST

The 1958 coup was led by two military leaders: General Abd al-Karim Qasim and Colonel Abd al-Salam Arif. Rather than establish order in the nation, their bloody action launched years of unrest and rule by military regimes. Qasim became the official head of Iraq and its prime minister. Supported by the military, he was an oppressive ruler who forbid organized politics and prevented civil and political activities he thought might challenge his authority. But in 1961, after Qasim failed to follow through on promises he had made to Iraqi Kurds to grant them more independence, the group rebelled. Their rebellion led other groups to resist as well. In 1963, Qasim's government was overthrown by members of a new political party—the Ba'th Party, or Arab Socialist Resurrection Party—and he was killed.

Iraq's government remained unsettled, as members of the Ba'th Party fought among themselves over political alignments with Egypt and Syria. The non-Ba'thist president, Abd al-Salam Arif, died in 1966 and was replaced by his brother. In 1968, the Ba'th Party overthrew the government and made Ahmad Hassan al-Bakr Iraq's new leader. Bakr shared power with the leader of the Ba'th Party, Saddam Hussein.

THE BA'TH PARTY

The Ba'th Party has several names, including the Arab Socialist Ba'th Party and the Arab Socialist Renaissance Party. In Arabic, the name is Hizb al-Ba'th al-'Arabi al-Ishtirakii.

The Ba'th Party was founded in 1943 in Damascus, the capital of Syria. The party joined with the Syrian Socialist Party in 1953 and became the Arab Socialist Ba'th Party. The party opposed colonialism and imperialism, and it was influenced by Islam. The party divided in the 1960s, the decade in which Ba'thists took power in Syria and in Iraq. Ba'thists faced opposition in both countries: the Muslim Brotherhood in Syria and the Kurds and the Shiites in Iraq. The Iraq faction of the Ba'th Party was removed from power in 2003.

SADDAM HUSSEIN, DICTATOR

After Bakr resigned, Hussein became president on July 16, 1979. He had other titles as well: secretary-general of the Ba'th Party, commander in chief, and chairman of the Revolutionary Command Council. A brutal leader, Hussein ruled through force and intimidation.

The years of Hussein's rule were marked by fighting, terror, and destruction. In 1979, the same year Hussein became president, a revolution occurred in Iran. Initially, Iraq supported Iran's new regime, but that support soon ended and the two countries went to war. Iraqi troops invaded Iran on September 22, 1980. The fighting lasted eight years, ending in 1988.

In the summer of 1990, Iraq's next conflict began. Iraq had long disputed the border with its neighbor Kuwait, arguing that some Kuwaiti land belonged to Iraq. Oil rights became another issue of conflict. Iraq claimed Kuwait was overproducing the valuable commodity—a major export for Iraq—and thus driving down the price.

On August 2, 1990, Iraq invaded Kuwait. Iraqi troops swarmed the capital and took over the government. The UN responded immediately by condemning the action. Four days later, on August 6, the UN imposed economic sanctions on Iraq. UN member nations ceased trading with Iraq, cutting it off financially in an effort to force Hussein to remove his

Saddam Hussein, 2002

UN SANCTIONS

On August 2, 1990, the UN Security Council passed Resolution 660, which condemned Iraq's invasion of Kuwait and called for Iraqi troops to withdraw immediately. When Saddam Hussein did not oblige, the UN Security Council passed Resolution 661, which put a hold on trade between UN members and Iraq. This trade embargo severely damaged Iraq's economy, and many Iraqis suffered during this economic downturn. Food was rationed, unemployment rose, inflation increased, and public services such as education were cut.

In 1991, the UN passed resolutions to help the Iraqi people, creating an oil-for-food program that allowed Iraq to sell a certain amount of oil to allow it to buy necessities such as food and medicine. Iraq refused the offer, which required allowing weapons inspections. The Iraqi people continued to suffer, especially children, who were particularly hard hit by food shortages and health crises. The program was the result of UN observations that "the Iraqi people may soon face a further imminent catastrophe, which could include epidemic and famine, if massive life-supporting needs are not rapidly met."[1]

Five years later, in 1996, Iraq finally agreed to work with the UN. In December, Iraq began exporting oil again. Three months later, Iraq received its first shipments of food and medicine.

troops from Kuwait. But the tactic did not work. Hussein refused to give up Kuwait, and on August 8, Iraq claimed Kuwait as its own.

The UN gave Iraq a deadline of January 15, 1991, to withdraw its troops. US troops were quickly moved into the Persian Gulf and stationed in Saudi Arabia. By late February, Hussein had not complied with the UN's request, and so a military coalition of troops from more than two dozen countries, led by the United States, joined in Operation Desert Storm and drove Iraqi forces out of Kuwait. For three more years, Iraq refused to officially acknowledge Kuwait as independent or to accept its borders.

The oil fields of Kuwait burned during the war.

After the conflict, the UN imposed several inspection requirements on the defeated nation. The UN wanted to inspect Iraq for components for nuclear weapons and a variety of ballistic, biological, and chemical weapons. Iraq resisted UN inspection, however, and the UN embargoes continued.

A few years later, conflict erupted again within Iraq. Kurds rebelled in the north, and Shiites rebelled in the south. Hussein's government put down both uprisings. Iraq's relations with the West continued to be tense because of the ongoing economic sanctions. In addition, Iraq still refused to let the UN conduct weapons inspections.

The tension erupted, and on December 16, 1998, US and British forces began bombing Iraq's weapons areas. The air strikes lasted four days. Disagreements over weapons inspections in Iraq continued. In early 2001, the United States and the United Kingdom launched another round of air attacks against Iraq.

THE WAR IN IRAQ

Tensions between Iraq and the United States grew as the Iraqis continued resisting weapons inspections. The attacks of September 11, 2001, on New York City and Washington DC renewed Americans' fears about unstable nations having weapons of mass destruction (WMDs). In early 2003, the United States and the United Kingdom declared war on Iraq. The UN was divided on the issue, but that did not prevent the US and British governments from challenging Hussein. On March 20, the United States, the United Kingdom, and their allies began air attacks on Iraq. Then, a coalition of US-led troops invaded on the ground. Those forces took control of Baghdad on April 9, and Hussein fled. The fall of Hussein did not end Iraq's troubles, however. Looting, riots, and chaos took hold, and insurgents began a guerilla war that killed coalition troops and Iraqi bystanders alike.

Hussein was captured in December 2003. He was tried for war crimes against his people in 2005, found guilty, and executed in December 2006. The WMDs that US President George W. Bush had been certain were in Iraq were never found. However, coalition forces did discover the mass graves of countless Iraqis that Hussein was responsible for killing.

Sectarian groups began fighting for control over the country. The bloodshed peaked in 2006. Bush sent an additional 20,000 US troops to Iraq in 2007.[2] US forces and Iraqi groups worked together to establish order, and the alliance began having positive results. Casualties in Baghdad finally began decreasing by the end of the year, and it seemed the

HUSSEIN'S CAPTURE, TRIAL, AND DEATH

After the US-led coalition forces invaded Baghdad and took over Iraq's government in early 2003, Saddam Hussein went into hiding. Troops spent many months searching for the former dictator. Then on December 13, US troops captured Hussein north of Baghdad, near Tikrit, his birthplace on the banks of the Tigris.

The soldiers surrounded a two-room hut situated between two farmhouses. The simple home provided access to an underground hideout, which was hidden by dirt and a rug. Hussein did not resist arrest.

In October 2005, Hussein went on trial in Iraq. He and several others were charged with killing almost 150 citizens of the town of Al-Dujayl in 1982. The trial lasted nine months, and the Iraqi High Tribunal adjourned in July 2006. In November, Hussein was found guilty of several offenses, including killing, illegal imprisonment, and torture. In December, he was sentenced to death. Hussein was executed by hanging on December 30.

situation was stabilizing. However, attacks continued and uncertainty remained.

Iraq continued to experience great turmoil after becoming an independent nation in the first half of the twentieth century, and the first few years of the new millennium proved no different. But the instability caused by the war in Iraq brought about a new government. This new leadership has the potential to create a strong, productive nation. The war also revealed the resiliency of the Iraqi people.

US troops remove a statue of Saddam Hussein after the capture of Baghdad.

CHAPTER 5

PEOPLE: VARIED AND DEVOTED

The Arab invasions that occurred well over 1,000 years ago greatly influenced Iraq's population and culture. Today, two ethnic groups dominate Iraqi culture: the Arabs and the Kurds. Between 75 and 80 percent of Iraqis are Arab, and between 15 and 20 percent are Kurdish. The remaining population, approximately 5 percent, consists of Turkmens, Assyrians, and members of other minorities such as Armenians.[1]

In mid-2011, the estimated population of Iraq was almost 30.4 million people, making it the thirty-ninth most populous country in the world. The life expectancy in Iraq averages 70.55 years: 69.15 for men and 72.02 for women. Iraq ranks one hundred forty fifth in the world for life expectancy.[2]

Most Iraqis are Arabs and Muslims.

LANGUAGES

A handful of languages are spoken in Iraq. There are two official languages: Arabic and Kurdish, which is the official language in Kurdish areas. Other languages include Turkic, Assyrian, and Armenian.

Languages are traced through trees, similar to how people trace their ancestry. Arabic is a southern-central Semitic language spoken in

YOU SAY IT!

English	Iraqi Arabic
Hello	'as-salaamu 'alaykum (ah-sah-lah-moh ah-lay-koom)
Good morning	Sabaah al-khayr (sah-bah ahl-kah-yehr)
Good evening	Masaa' al-khayr (mah-sah ahl-kah-yehr)
Excuse me	'afwan (af-wahn)
Thank you	shukran (shook-ran)

This tile shows "Allah" written in Arabic script.

many countries. It is the language of the Arabian Peninsula, the Middle East, and northern Africa. It falls into the larger classification of Afro-Asiatic languages. Arabic is the language of the Koran, Islam's holy book. Classical Arabic is the literary Arabic found in the Koran, whereas colloquial Arabic is the language spoken throughout the Islamic world. There are many dialects of colloquial Arabic, including those of Arabia, Egypt, Iraq, North Africa, and Syria.

The Kurdish language developed from a different branch of linguistics. It is a West Iranian language that is part of the Indo-European group. It also has several dialects. The two main dialect groups are the northern and the central. In Iraq, the official form of Kurdish is Kurdi. It has multiple subdialects, including Kermanshahi, Leki, Gurani, and Zaza.

Many Iraqis are bilingual, especially minorities who speak both Arabic and the language of their culture. In addition, English is commonly spoken in the business sector.

ETHNIC GROUPS

Hospitality is an important part of Arabic culture, and Iraqi hosts want to make guests feel welcome.

Arabs comprise the largest group of Iraqis. Many Arabs are descendents of tribes that moved to the region centuries ago. Some tribes came to the land that is now Iraq looking for water. Others came with the spread of Islam, and still others came even before the birth of Muhammad, the founder of Islam. Although the many tribes were once distinct, today, they are united by religion and language. Arabs tend to practice Islam and speak Arabic. Family is important to Arabs, and a single house may be home to several generations. Familial bonds often extend beyond the immediate family to include the tribe.

Traditionally, a tribe's structure includes multiple levels. The *khams* is the basic unit of the structure and the most important. It includes the extended family and consists of the male members who have the same great-great grandfather. A *biet*, or house, is comparable to a khams. Multiple biets join to form a *fakhdh*, or clan. Clans come together to create an *ashira*, which is a tribal organization. Finally, the largest level of the tribal structure is the *qabila*, a confederation of tribes. There are several major tribal confederations in Iraq, including Shammar, Dulaym, Jibur, Tikriti-al, al-Khaza'il, Anizah, Banu Hushaim, al-Aqrah, al-Zubayd, and Ubayd. These groups vary in size, reaching more than 1 million members. The Shammar may have more than 1.5 million people. These groups also have varied histories and origins. The Anizah are the world's largest group of nomadic Arabs, and the Ubayd descend from a people that settled along the Tigris River in the sixth century. Seventy-five percent of Iraqis are members of a tribe or are related to a tribe.[3]

The Kurds, Iraq's second-largest population, reside in Kurdistan, an area in Iraq's mountainous north that extends beyond the nation's borders into Armenia, Iran, Syria, and Turkey. The Kurds have their own culture and language, Kurdish, although most speak Arabic as well. Traditionally, the Kurds and others in this region were sheep and goat herders and farmers who lived in rural villages. Today, most Kurds live

THE KURDISH STRUGGLE

The Kurdish people have struggled for cultural and political independence since the early twentieth century, when they aspired to establish their own state after World War I. The British ruled Iraq at the time and put down the attempt. Over the years, the Kurds have continued to seek independence.

Iraqi Kurdistan was given increased autonomy in the 1970s, but only on paper. In the 1980s, Saddam Hussein had 4,000 Kurdish villages destroyed. In November 1991, 100,000 people were expelled from Kirkuk, and by 2001, at least 600,000 people had been displaced. But the Kurdish people did not give up their fight. Since 1991, the Kurdistan Regional Government has rebuilt more than 2,500 of the destroyed villages with the help of nongovernmental organizations and UN agencies.[4]

The new Iraqi constitution, ratified in October 2005, acknowledges Iraqi Kurdistan as its own region that includes the governorates of Arbil, Dahuk, and Al-Sulaymaniyyah. Kurdistan is autonomous in several ways. It has its own border with Iraq, its own economy, and some control over its own foreign policy. In fact, the Kurdish government has been acknowledged internationally. Kurdish political leaders do not report to Baghdad, and the Kurds police themselves.

and work in the cities of Arbil, Dahuk, and Al-Sulaymaniyyah. Rather than herd and farm, they work in construction, government, and trade.

Other groups also call Iraq home, including a handful of minorities. The Madan, for example, are Shiites who live in the marshes of southern Iraq. The Bedouin are a nomadic people who often live in the desert and herd animals. The Lur people live near the Iranian border and speak an Iranian language. Armenian Iraqis live mostly in the nation's capital, although some also reside in northern Iraq. Three additional minority groups also inhabit the north: Turks, Turkmen, and Assyrians.

Kurdish families, Arbil, Iraq

AN URBAN POPULATION

Iraqis are predominantly an urban people. In 2008, 67 percent of the population lived in cities. Iraq's five largest cities—Baghdad, Mosul, Arbil, Basra, and Al-Sulaymaniyyah—are home to more than 30 percent of Iraqis. With more than 5.7 million residents, Baghdad has the largest population.[5]

Numerous towns and villages dot the nation's landscape. Thousands of smaller communities with between 100 and 2,000 houses are spread across much of Iraq.[6] Most of them are located near the Tigris and Euphrates Rivers. In these communities, the inhabitants mostly farm.

Villages in the north are mostly Kurdish, and those in the south tend to be Madan. The Madan have suffered with the loss of the marshlands in southern Iraq, and many have left the area. The nation's more arid regions were once inhabited by Bedouin nomads, but their numbers have dwindled.

IRAQ'S LARGEST CITIES, 2009

- Baghdad: 5.751 million
- Mosul: 1.447 million
- Arbil: 1.009 million
- Basra: 923,000
- Al-Sulaymaniyyah: 836,000[7]

The Tigris River runs through Baghdad, Iraq's largest city.

RELIGION

Iraq is an Islamic nation. The constitution designates Islam as the official religion, and laws are not allowed to contradict Islamic law. However, the Iraqi constitution does guarantee religious freedom for people of other faiths. Ninety-seven percent of Iraqis are Muslim. Approximately two-thirds of Iraq's Muslims are Shiite and one-third are Sunni.[8]

Both groups follow the Koran and the teachings of Muhammad. The sects differ in their beliefs regarding the religion's early history and the Mahdi, the Muslim messiah or savior. Most Shiites live in central and southern Iraq, and most Sunnis reside in central and northern Iraq. The biggest issue between the two factions, which are often in conflict, is

ISLAMIC RELIGIOUS SITES

Iraq is home to many Islamic religious sites. Some are important to Sunnis, others are important to Shiites, and still others are important to both sects. Baghdad, for example, was a center of Islamic learning for many years.

The two most important holy cities for Shiites are located in Iraq. Al-Najaf and Karbala are both in southern Iraq. Al-Najaf is believed to be the resting place of one of the sect's most revered figures, Ali (600–661 CE). Ali was the cousin and son-in-law of Muhammad, the founder of Islam. Other important religious sites include Kufah and Samarra, both south of Baghdad.

Baghdad is home to an important Sunni site: Abu Hanifah Mosque. It was built around the tomb of Abu Hanifah (699–767 CE), a Muslim jurist and theologian. He formalized Islamic legal codes.

Saint Joseph Church in Arbil. A small minority of Iraqis are Christian.

JEWS IN IRAQ

The Jewish people have a long history in Iraq. Jews began inhabiting the area that is now Iraq more than 2,000 years ago. When the Assyrians defeated northern tribes of Israel in 722 BCE and the Babylonians defeated southern tribes in 586 BCE, defeated Jews were brought back to Iraq—many as slaves. By the early twentieth century CE, one-third of Baghdad's inhabitants were Jewish. By the mid-1930s, the Jewish population reached approximately 120,000.[10]

But conditions began changing for the Jews when they were persecuted during World War II. In June 1941, 180 Jewish people were murdered and nearly 1,000 were wounded in Iraq as the result of pro-Nazi rioting and violence. From 1949 to 1951, 124,000 Jewish people left Iraq, many relocating to the new Jewish state of Israel.[11] In 1952, the Iraqi government prohibited Jews from moving out of the country.

After the Ba'thists took control in the 1960s, life became increasingly difficult for Jews in Iraq and included the threat of death by torture and hanging. The Jewish population continued to decline. In 2004, approximately three dozen Jews lived in Baghdad. By 2008, this number had dwindled to the single digits. Those Jews who remained claimed they were simply too old to move.

political power. Sunnis have held Iraq's highest offices since it officially became a country, despite the fact that the Sunni population is considerably smaller than the Shiite population.

Three percent of the Iraqi people follow other faiths, including Christianity and Judaism.[9] Iraq's Jews have a long history in the region, which traces back to the country's very beginnings in Mesopotamia.

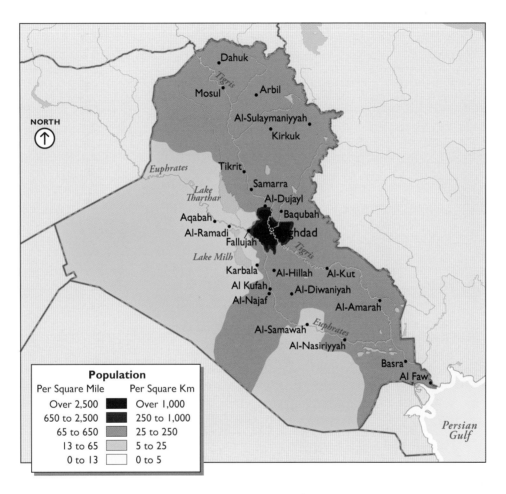

Population

Per Square Mile		Per Square Km
Over 2,500		Over 1,000
650 to 2,500		250 to 1,000
65 to 650		25 to 250
13 to 65		5 to 25
0 to 13		0 to 5

Population Density of Iraq

CHAPTER 6

CULTURE: MIDDLE EAST MEETS WEST

Because Iraq is an Islamic nation, daily life is punctuated by calls to prayer. The *adhan*, or "announcement," calls Muslims to *salat*, or daily prayer, five times each day—dawn, noon, afternoon, sunset, and evening—and to public worship on Friday. The muezzin, a servant of the mosque, calls Muslims to prayer.

Whereas most Iraqis are Muslim, a very small number practice other faiths. But Iraqis are much more than their religion. Iraq's culture has many other aspects, including the arts with which Iraqis express themselves, the holidays and festivals they celebrate together, the foods they prepare and enjoy, the sports they cheer, and the buildings they construct.

Celil Hayat Mosque in Arbil. Much of Iraqi culture is shaped by Islam.

ARTS AND CRAFTS

Iraq's long history of creativity includes handicrafts such as pottery. The Sumerians developed the pottery wheel, and for millennia, talented Iraqis have created pottery that is both beautiful and utilitarian. For example, a *habb al-maa* is a large clay pot for keeping water. In addition to pots, craftspeople create decorative tiles.

Another artistic tradition in Iraq is weaving, made famous by the wool rugs often referred to as Persian or Oriental. Many women in Iraq make these rugs, spending hours bringing colorful, intricate patterns to life. Other

BASRA'S POTTERY INDUSTRY AT RISK

In the ninth century, Basra potters created styles and techniques of pottery making that changed the medium. They invented glazes in bold, bright cobalt blue and used a new method of firing the clay that created a metallic iridescence. But today, the city's pottery industry is suffering and appears to be heading toward extinction.

Iraqi News reported on the issue in January 2008, telling the story of Umm Salem, who wanted to buy a water pot but could not find one in Basra. Salem had to ask someone in Baghdad to buy her a *habb al-maa*. Hajj Jabbar Shanshoul has sold pottery for more than 50 years. He explained the decrease in potters: "Many pottery stores have changed their trade because of the high costs of transport between Baghdad and Basra, which negatively affected the price of their goods."[1] The pots, once the only way to keep water cool, have been largely replaced by refrigerators.

skilled artisans make baskets and leather goods. Yet others work with wood, making backgammon boards, chess sets, and musical instruments.

Making musical instruments is a successful industry in Kurdistan, where there is a good supply of the wood needed to create high-quality instruments. In addition, the success of this industry reflects the importance of music to the Kurds, who take pride in their musical traditions.

MUSIC AND DANCE

Music and dance are valued throughout Iraq. The nation's many tribes and cultures have unique heritages that are celebrated with traditional singing and dancing. For example, a musical concept called the *maqam* characterizes the Arabic songs traditional in Iraq and in broader areas of the Middle East and northern Africa. The maqam is a set of tones and specific patterns for combining them, and it involves pitches and melodies not typical in Western music. Whereas Western music uses half and whole tones, the maqam uses these tones plus tones between them. Using this set of tones helps create the emotional quality often associated with traditional Iraqi music.

It is considered rude to point with one finger or make an "okay" or "thumbs-up" hand sign.

The lyrics of Iraqi music often come from Arabic poetry. The music is played on a variety of instruments, including drums, harps, lutes, lyres, ouds, and *rebabas*. All but the drums are stringed instruments of different shapes

that are plucked or strummed. Some of the modern instruments used by musicians today produce sounds that are more controlled and specific than those of traditional instruments. These new instruments miss some of the in-between tones that are unique to the maqam, resulting somewhat in the loss of this traditional Iraqi and Middle Eastern music.

Iraqis enjoy imported elements of Western culture including ballet, classical music, and theater. In addition, jazz music, introduced by Americans, has made its way into classical Iraqi music through artists such as Amir El Saffar, who has helped create Iraqi jazz.

Access to these new arts as well as traditional

A musician plays an oud.

IRAQ'S BALLET SCHOOL

Iraq has an arts school devoted to music and ballet. Founded in 1967, the Music and Ballet School of Baghdad teaches school-age children and today provides a creative haven from the city's war-torn streets. But enrollment in the school has dropped. Groups have challenged the school because they oppose females exposing their skin in the presence of males, which dancers do when dressed in a leotard. Other groups oppose music in general. Strong threats have been made against the school and the children, and one child was kidnapped and ransomed. However, the students and teachers persevere in the face of these difficulties.

Musical appreciation and performance occur at a professional level in Iraq's National Symphony Orchestra and National Ballet. Most members of the symphony are former students of the Music and Ballet School, which serves to inspire the nation's young music students.

cultural events has been hampered by the years of poverty and upheaval in Iraq. Still, Iraqis continue to enjoy music and have favorite performers, including oudist Naseer Shamma, singer Nazem al-Ghazali, and singer and guitarist Ilham Al Madfai.

LITERATURE, THEATER, AND FILM

Iraq has an extensive literary history. The Sumerians developed cuneiform, the first-known written language, and writing has continued to thrive in the region, particularly poetry. Several modern poets have reached prominence worldwide. Nazik al-Mala'ika, who died in 2007, was a prominent female poet in the Arab world. Muhammad Mahdi al-Jawahiri, who died in 1997, was considered the last master of neoclassical Arabic poetry. Publishing suffered in Iraq because of the war, but it has shown signs of recovery.

Iraq has an array of media, including a national television service, regional television stations (one broadcasting in Kurdish), and several newspapers. The top Arabic papers are *Al-Thawrah, Al-Irāq*, and *Al-Jumhūriyyah*.

Iraqis also have a history of enjoying theater and film, even though doing so declined during the war. After closing its doors for more than six years, the Iraq National Theater reopened in October 2009.

The movie industry has also suffered in Iraq. Because of the war, Iraqis stopped producing films and going to movies. During the industry's peak in the 1940s, a series of popular romantic musicals were made, and today, these movies, along with those created since, are in need of restoration. Filmmaker Oday Rasheed is leading the effort to save his country's film heritage. His movie *Underexposure* was Iraq's first postwar feature film, and in 2005, it won the award for best film at the Singapore Film Festival. Rasheed is working with another director, Mohamed al-Daradji, to create an Iraqi film production center.

SPORTS

As in most other Arab nations, the favorite sport in Iraq is soccer. For many Iraqis, it has reached the level of a national passion. Soccer grew in popularity after 1980, serving as a distraction from the nation's economic

WOMEN IN SOCIETY

Iraqi society has tended to be patriarchal and conservative, particularly in rural areas. In this society, women often have not had the same rights as men. That changed somewhat in the 1970s, however, when the government passed laws that gave women significant advances in the areas of economics, education, and politics. Other laws regarding marriage made it impossible for a Muslim husband to divorce his wife simply by declaring they were divorced, which had long been an accepted practice. In addition, women received greater rights regarding child custody when separating from or divorcing their husbands.

Iraqi women can vote. They can also run for office, although many are criticized for doing so. A government quota specifies that men can hold only 75 percent of the seats in parliament, which means that at least 25 percent of the members are female. Unfortunately, the women who do become members of parliament tend not to be taken seriously because many men perceive them as simply filling the quota.

Fans celebrate Iraq's win over North Korea
in soccer's Asian Cup in January 2011.

and political struggles. Today, a huge crowd of Iraqis waits outside Baghdad's Al-Sha'b Stadium during games—even after the last seat has been occupied—and millions of other devoted fans watch on television. Iraqis were rewarded when their team won the 2007 Asian Cup.

Other Iraqi athletes have competed in the Olympic Summer Games. Iraqi athletes debuted in the 1948 games, and they made their second appearance in 1960. At the 1960 games, Iraq won its first medal when Abdul Wahid Aziz took home a bronze in weight lifting.

HOLIDAYS AND FESTIVALS

The people of Iraq celebrate many events each year, including religious and secular holidays. Secular, or nonreligious, holidays include New Year's Day and Army Day in January, Labor Day in May, Republic Day in July, and Ceasefire Day in August.

Religious holidays are extremely important to the Islamic nation. Islamic holy days and festivals include Eid al-Fitr, Eid al-Adha, Ashura, and the Islamic New Year. Eid al-Fitr, or the Festival of Breaking Fast, is a celebration marking the end of Ramadan, a month in which Muslims abstain from eating, drinking, smoking, and participating in fun activities during the day. Eid al-Adha, or the Festival of Sacrifice, commemorates the passage from the Koran that tells of Abraham's willingness to sacrifice Ishmael, his son, to obey God. Rather than allow Abraham to

Traditionally, meals are served on the floor in Iraqi homes.

sacrifice his beloved son, God gave him a ram to sacrifice instead. Muslims celebrate by sacrificing their own animal, such as a goat, sheep, or camel. Ashura is a day of mourning for Iraqi Shiites that honors the martyrdom of the Prophet's grandson Hussain. It is also observed by some Arab and Kurdish Sunnis.

The dates of Iraq's secular holidays are consistent, but those of the Islamic holy days are not. The Islamic calendar is lunar based, which means it has 12 months, each beginning around the time of the new moon. The variance in this calendar causes the days of the celebrations to change from year to year.

CUISINE

Iraq's cuisine is similar to that of other Middle Eastern countries, including Lebanon and Syria, and it has been influenced by the cuisine of Turkey and Iran. Like many Middle Easterners, Iraqis enjoy chicken and lamb. These meats are often marinated with lemon, garlic, and spices and then grilled. It also common to cook meat with fruit, which is done in kibbe, a popular dish of minced meat, nuts, raisins, and spices. Fish is also popular among Iraqis. However, pork is forbidden to Muslims.

Rice and bread are staples in the Iraqi diet. Pita, or pocket bread, is popular in Iraq and other Middle Eastern countries. Another favorite is *sambusak*, a crescent-shaped bread that consists of dough stuffed with meat or cheese. Fruits and vegetables are dietary staples as well,

especially dates. They are abundant in Iraq and often served with coffee
at the end of a meal.

ARCHITECTURE

The most striking structure in Iraq's architecture is the mosque. Domes
and minarets—the familiar elements of mosque design—mark village and
city skylines across the country. Some have golden domes that shine in

the Iraqi sun. Others have intricate designs in rich colors, especially blues and greens. Within each mosque is a prayer room. Many mosques also have a large, open courtyard.

Throughout the country are ancient structures and archaeological ruins. The most important sites are Ashur, Babylon, Hatra, Khorsabad, Nimrud, Nineveh, Samarra, and Ur. Ashur was the religious capital of Assyria. Writings show the city had approximately 36 temples to honor the gods, although only a fraction of them have been discovered. Remnants of three palaces have also been unearthed, as have the walls that protected the city. Nimrud, another Assyrian city, was a royal military capital. In addition to discovering temples and walls there, archaeologists have found many religious texts, treaties, and ivory carvings. These carvings, numbering in the thousands, now comprise one of the greatest ivory collections in the world. Babylon has interested archaeologists and tourists alike. This city is mentioned in the Bible and was the home of the famous hanging gardens, one of the seven wonders of the ancient world.

Much of Iraq's architecture has been damaged during the war. This is particularly true in Baghdad, where the fighting was fierce.

Baghdad's Martyr's Monument was built in remembrance of those who died in the 1980s war with Iran.

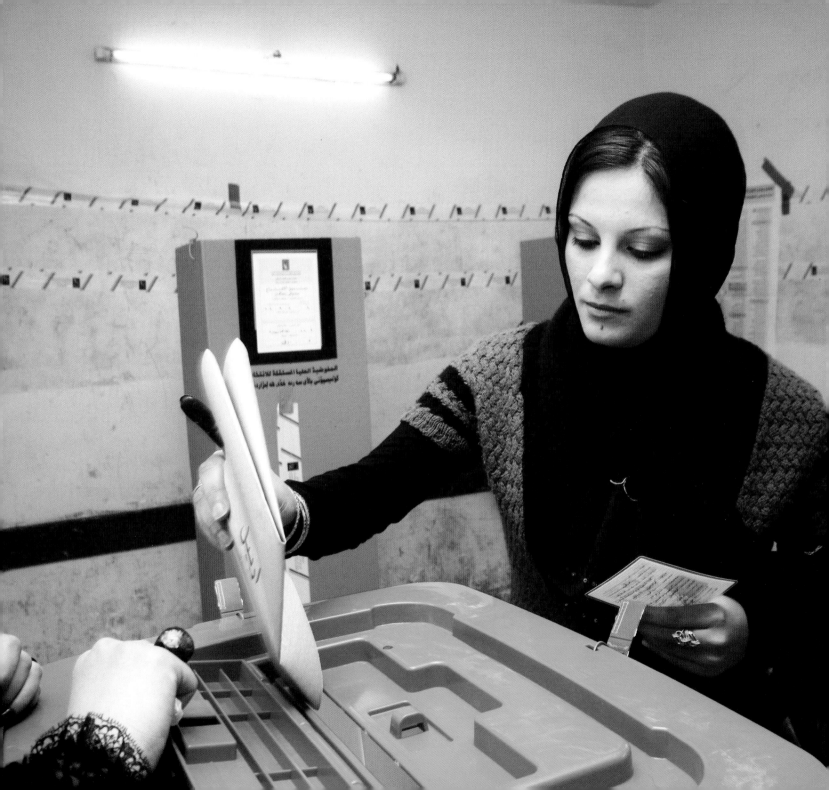

CHAPTER 7

POLITICS:
STARTING OVER

Iraq's political situation has historically been one of turmoil and uncertainty. When coalition forces overthrew Hussein and his Ba'th government in the spring of 2003, they put in place the Coalition Provisional Authority (CPA). The CPA worked to improve security, rebuild infrastructure, and design a new government, but its control was shaky. It faced a growing insurgency, violence from terrorist groups, and political disagreement along sectarian lines. The minority Sunnis, who had controlled the country under Hussein's regime, feared a loss of power to the Shiite majority, led by Ayatollah Ali al-Sistani. In the north, Kurds and Sunnis fought for control.

In 1980, women in Iraq gained the right to vote and run for office.

A woman votes in the 2010 Iraqi general election.

Iraq's flag has three colors divided into equal-sized horizontal sections, or bands. The top band is red and represents overcoming challenges through a bloody fight. The middle band is white and represents a bright future. The bottom band is black and represents oppression. Centered in the white band and written in green Arabic script is the Takbir, *Allahu akbar*. The Takbir is an Arabic expression that means "God is great."

Iraq's flag is similar to the flags of other Middle Eastern nations. The flags of Iraq, Egypt, Syria, and Yemen all have the same three bands of color. All are based on the Arab Liberation flag, which has the pattern of red, white, and black. The white band differs from flag to flag. In place of the Takbir, Egypt's flag has a gold eagle, Syria's flag has two stars, and Yemen's flag has white space.

The design of Iraq's flag has changed throughout the years. The current flag was adopted in 2008 and is similar in design to one adopted in 1963. In that flag, three green stars appeared in the band of white, not the Takbir. In 1991, Saddam Hussein added the Takbir, interspersing the two words between the three stars.

FIRST ELECTIONS

In the summer of 2003, the CPA appointed 25 Iraqis to the Iraqi Governing Council (IGC). Although the IGC had limited power at that time, it was assigned the important task of developing an interim constitution, which it completed in March 2004. In 2004, the nation also began preparing for its first elections in decades. On January 30, 2005, Iraq held three elections. Iraqis nationwide voted for a National Assembly of 275 members. Iraqis in the Kurdish region voted for a Kurdish National Assembly of 105 members. And in each of Iraq's 18 provinces, citizens voted for

Flag of Iraq

NATIONAL ANTHEM

Iraq's national anthem is "Mawtini," and it was adopted in 2004, following the removal of Saddam Hussein. The title is Arabic for "My Homeland." "Mawtini" is a popular folk tune in the Middle East, and it is also the unofficial anthem of the Palestinians. The anthem has three verses, each beginning and ending with "My homeland, my homeland." The anthem begins with the following verse:

My homeland, my homeland

Glory and beauty, sublimity and splendor

Are in your hills, are in your hills

Life and deliverance, pleasure and hope

Are in your air, are in your Air

Will I see you? Will I see you?

Safe and comforted, sound and honored

Safe and comforted, sound and honored

Will I see you in your eminence?

Reaching to the stars, reaching to the stars

My homeland, my homeland[3]

representatives to fill seats in local government.[1]

Any Iraqi citizen age 18 years or older could vote, which meant more than 14 million people went to the polls. In addition, another 1 million Iraqis living outside Iraq were eligible to vote.[2] Dozens of candidates were up for election, including women. Every candidate had to be at least 30 years old, and none could be a former member of the Ba'th Party, the armed forces, or a party with a militia—all of which had been banned from the elections. After casting ballots, many Iraqis left the polls proudly waving their index fingers, which had been dipped in purple ink to show they had voted.

The elections put the Shiite majority in power. Despite the hopes of the people for stability, violence between Shiites and Sunnis escalated. Bombs rocked Baghdad daily, and millions fled the country. Iraq had a new government, but it was still unable to provide security for its people.

IRAQ'S CONSTITUTION

The members of the National Assembly had the primary goal of drafting a new constitution by August 15, 2005. Two months later, on October 15, Iraqis approved the new constitution by majority vote.

Iraq's constitution begins with a preamble that acknowledges Iraqis' history and strong faith. The preamble also addresses the goals of the people and reflects the hope many Iraqis have for the future:

> *We the people of Iraq of all components and shades have taken upon ourselves to decide freely and with our choice to unite our future and to take lessons from yesterday for tomorrow, to draft, through the values and ideals of the heavenly messages and the findings of science and man's civilization, this lasting constitution. The adherence to this constitution preserves for Iraq its free union, its people, its land and its sovereignty.[4]*

Approximately 2 million Iraqis fled during the war; most are now refugees in Syria and Jordan.

Iraq's new constitution outlines several features of the nation and its new government. The first section addresses fundamental principles, including religion, language, the capital, the flag, and holy shrines and religious sites. The second section details civil and political rights. The third section defines the organization of the government, and the fourth explains the federal government's powers.

The fifth section outlines the powers of the regions and acknowledges Kurdistan as a federal region. The final section of the new constitution explains how the government functioned during the transition before the election and lays out rules for changing the constitution in the future.

The new Iraqi constitution allows no laws to contradict the laws of Islam.

By the end of 2005, Iraq had a new constitution and a new, permanent parliament. Yet the insurgency continued. Finally, in 2007, conditions began to change, and by 2008—five years after the war in Iraq had begun—the level of violence had dropped dramatically. The underlying causes of the violence—religious and sectarian tensions—remained unresolved, however.

SYSTEM OF GOVERNMENT

Iraq's new government is a parliamentary democracy. The government has three branches: executive, legislative, and judicial.

The executive branch encompasses multiple offices. The president is the chief of state. He or she is elected by the legislature to a four-year

The Iraqi parliament meets in a Baghdad convention center until its own building can be constructed.

term and can be reelected to a second term. Jalal Talabani was elected president of Iraq by the National Assembly in April 2005. A year later, he was elected president again under the new constitution, and in November 2010, he was reelected again. In 2011, Iraq increased its count of vice presidents from two to three. However, shortly after the change, one of the original vice presidents resigned. Together, the president and vice presidents form the Presidency Council. Iraq's prime minister is the head of government. Nuri al-Maliki became prime minister in May 2006.

STRUCTURE OF THE GOVERNMENT OF IRAQ

Executive Branch	Legislative Branch	Judicial Branch
President (head of state) and Vice Presidents Prime minister (head of government) and Deputy Prime Ministers Council of Ministers	Council of Representatives (lower house) The constitution calls for creation of an upper house, the Federation Council.	Higher Judicial Council Federal Supreme Court Federal Court of Cassation Public Prosecution Department Judiciary Oversight Commission

There are three deputy prime ministers: Husayn al-Shahristani, Salih al-Mutlaq, and Rowsch Nuri Shaways. The Presidency Council appoints 43 ministers to the Council of Ministers, which includes the prime minister and deputy prime ministers.

The federal government also has a unicameral legislative branch. The Council of Representatives has 325 members who elect the president and help create Iraq's federal laws. In 2010, the members represented a number of parties. These political parties claimed the following number of seats: Iraqi National Movement, 91; State of Law Coalition, 89; Iraqi National Alliance, 70; Kurdistan Alliance, 43; Goran (Change) List, 8;

Nuri al-Maliki became prime minister of Iraq in 2006.

Tawafuq Front, 6; Iraqi Unity Alliance, 4; Kurdistan Islamic Union, 4; and Kurdistan Islamic Group, 2. In addition, 8 seats were reserved for minorities.[5]

POLITICAL PARTIES OF IRAQ

Iraqi National Movement: This is a coalition party that includes several member groups. It is a secular party and its unity depends on the charisma of its leaders.

Iraqi National Alliance: This party is predominately Shiite. It is a coalition of several smaller parties that take different positions on a number of issues, including the role of the centralized government.

Kurdistan Alliance: Iraq's president, Jalal Talabani, belongs to this party. It is a Kurdish party that has not tried to include other ethnic groups. It also controls the regional government in Kurdistan.

State of Law Coalition: This is the party of Iraq's prime minister, Nuri al-Maliki. The party has begun a transition from a Shiite party to a secular, nationalist party. It is unified by Maliki, who has a strong personality.

The Council of Representatives controls the Federation Council, a group that will consist of representatives from Iraq's provinces and other local jurisdictions. The 2005 constitution called for the creation of this council, which has not yet come into being.

The final branch of Iraq's new government is the judicial branch. This branch of government has several levels, including the Higher Judicial Council, the Federal Supreme Court, the Federal Court of Cassation, the Public Prosecution Department, and the Judiciary Oversight

Commission. The members of this governmental branch are appointed by the legislature and interpret Iraq's laws.

CHALLENGES

As Iraq moves forward with its new government and constitution, the longstanding divisions that have separated Iraqis for decades and even centuries remain in place. The challenge for Iraqis who have long defined themselves by certain tribes or sects—for example, as Kurds, Sunnis, or Shiites—is to look past these divisions and to work toward common goals. As history has shown, however, doing so is not easy.

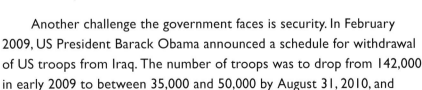

VIOLENCE AGAINST VOTERS

Iraq's elections have been marked by violence. In 2010, insurgents attacked voters at a polling place in an effort to intimidate them. Thirty-six people were killed, but the attacks did not keep voters from the polls. Police in Azamiyah, located in northern Iraq, reported at least 20 mortar attacks early in the day. But the bombing did not dissuade resident Walid Abid, who explained: "I am not scared and I am not going to stay put at home. Until when? We need to change things. If I stay home and [do] not come to vote, Azamiyah will get worse."[6] The incidents of violence against voters are examples of Iraq's ongoing struggle with security and with divisions among longstanding ethnic and sectarian groups, such as the Kurds, Shiites, and Sunnis.

Another challenge the government faces is security. In February 2009, US President Barack Obama announced a schedule for withdrawal of US troops from Iraq. The number of troops was to drop from 142,000 in early 2009 to between 35,000 and 50,000 by August 31, 2010, and then to none by December 31, 2011.[7] In April 2011, 47,000 US troops remained in Iraq.[8]

At that time, US Secretary of Defense Robert Gates visited Iraq to tell the country's leaders they would have to take swift action if they wanted to ask the United States to extend the deadline and keep US troops in the country for a longer period. Increasingly, the Iraqi government has been responsible for keeping the nation safe and secure.

Iraqi children gather to talk to a US soldier.

CHAPTER 8

ECONOMICS: WORKING TOWARD RECOVERY

The final decades of the twentieth century were economically challenging for Iraq. Trade sanctions against the nation during Saddam Hussein's regime seriously weakened its economy. But the new century has brought an improved economic situation as the value of the Iraqi dinar has improved steadily. Even so, the economic downturn that gripped the world beginning in 2008 limited the economic growth of most nations, making exporting a challenge. As Iraq continues to recover and build, its government must focus on improving the nation's economy, which heavily relies on the production of oil.

Lack of filling stations and infrastructure makes it difficult and expensive to buy gasoline in Iraq.

Iraq adopted a new design for its currency, the dinar, in 2003.

NATURAL RESOURCES AND CHIEF INDUSTRIES

As is true in many Middle Eastern countries, petroleum, or oil, plays a prominent role in Iraq's economy. It is Iraq's main natural resource, and the country ranks fourth in the world in proven oil reserves.[1] Not surprisingly, as the nation's greatest natural resource, oil is the backbone of Iraq's economy.

Oil production had decreased in recent decades as a result of Iraq's ongoing conflicts, but in recent years, production levels have begun to rebound. In fact, earnings from oil exports have returned to the level that existed before the most recent war. Moreover, exports are expected to continue to increase.

IRAQI OIL BY THE NUMBERS (2009 EST.)

Oil production: 2.399 million barrels/day
World rank: 12

Oil consumption: 687,000 barrels/day
World rank: 24

Oil exports: 1.91 million barrels/day
World rank: 11

Oil imports: 116,900 barrels/day
World rank: 59

Oil proven reserves (Jan. 2010 est.):
115 billion barrels
World rank: 4[2]

Iraq's economy is heavily dependent on oil.

In January 2011, exports exceeded 2 million barrels per day—a postwar record.[3]

In addition, natural gas, phosphates, sulfur, salt, steel, stone, and gypsum all contribute to industry in Iraq. Including oil production, industry accounts for the largest segment of the nation's income: 63 percent of the country's gross domestic product (GDP), which is the total value of goods produced in the country.[4] Chief industries include chemicals, construction materials, fertilizer, food processing, textiles, and metal fabrication and processing.

Another natural resource, although not in the traditional sense, is the Iraqi people. The service industry—which includes positions in government, businesses, banks, and offices—produces approximately 27 percent of Iraq's GDP.[5]

Crude oil is Iraq's greatest export. The nation also exports food, livestock, and crude materials other than fuel, which can include fruit oils, sand, gravel,

OPEC

Iraq is a founding member of the Organization of the Petroleum Exporting Countries (OPEC). Created in 1960 by Iran, Iraq, Kuwait, Saudi Arabia, and Venezuela, OPEC works to coordinate petroleum sales among its members to keep the price and supply of oil stable.

In 2011, OPEC members also included, in order of joining, Qatar (1961), Libya (1962), the United Arab Emirates (1967), Algeria (1969), Nigeria (1971), Ecuador (1973), and Angola (2007). In 2009, OPEC members held almost 80 percent of the world's crude oil reserves.[6]

A woman works to collect salt in Nippur.

unprocessed minerals, and unprocessed textile fibers, among other raw
materials. In 2009, the United States received the highest percentage of
Iraq's exports, more than 25 percent, followed by India, Italy, South Korea,
Taiwan, China, the Netherlands, and Japan. Iraq imports food, medicine,
and manufactured goods. Import partners include Turkey, Syria, the

United States, China, Jordan, and Italy. Turkey provides almost 25 percent of the items that Iraq imports.[7]

Increasing oil revenues have not solved Iraq's problems. The country struggles to use its resources effectively to rebuild infrastructure and improve human services. Corruption and theft result in the loss of billions of dollars.[8] In addition, Kurds and other minority groups fear that central government control of oil profits will cause them to lose their fair share of oil found on their lands.

AGRICULTURE

Today, agriculture accounts for less than 10 percent of Iraq's GDP. Approximately 13 percent of Iraq's land is arable, and it supports crops such as wheat, barley, rice, vegetables, fruit, tobacco, and cotton.[9] Dates are also grown in Iraq, which used to be the world's top producer of the fruit. However, as with many other things in Iraq, the date industry suffered as a result of war.

In 2006, Iraq spent approximately 8.6 percent of its GDP on its military.

Animals are also raised in Iraq. Ten percent of the country is permanent pasture, which is well suited to raising livestock such as cattle, sheep, and poultry. Fish are harvested as well, although there is no formal fishing industry. What fish are caught are mostly sold locally and thus do not affect the national economy.

Girls collecting dates, Qalatana, Iraq

TOURISM

Even though Iraq's history, culture, and landscape could make it an appealing tourist destination, the country has almost no tourism. The obvious reason is that it is dangerous to travel there. Visitors to Baghdad are primarily soldiers, diplomats, and journalists. In early 2011, the US State Department continued to discourage US citizens from traveling to Iraq.

According to the travel guide *Lonely Planet: Middle East*, Kurdistan is the only area of Iraq that is safe for travel. But not even that region is without risk. A particular threat is posed by land mines planted throughout the region during the war.

Once security improves dramatically, Iraqis and visitors alike will be able to travel freely and safely throughout Iraq. And at that point, the nation will have many opportunities for economic growth related to tourism. Thousands, if not millions, of people will likely want to visit many of Iraq's many ancient ruins. A prime example is Babylon, which the US government has provided $2 million to restore.[10]

INFRASTRUCTURE

Iraq once had one of the Middle East's best telecommunications networks, but today, services are limited and not very reliable. The nation's communications system needs repairs and upgrades. In addition, Iraq does not produce enough electricity, so electricity is rationed and blackouts are common. Aging and damaged water and sewage systems leave people without access to clean water and cause sanitation problems.

Iraqis have poor access to telephone, television, and radio—only 3 percent of homes have access to a telephone, 10 percent to a television, and 20 percent to a radio.[11] Some Iraqis do have access to cell phone service and the Internet. Cell phone service was banned by the Ba'ths, but it is now available in urban areas, as is Internet access. In 2009, approximately 1.1 million Iraqis had landline telephones and 19.7 million had cell phones.[12]

Transportation in Iraq is quite varied. Some Iraqis still rely on ancient modes

PRESERVING THE HISTORY, GROWING THE ECONOMY

In 2011, Iraq began restoration efforts at Babylon, one of its ancient cities. Iraq is home to several such remarkable sites, and the risk of losing these historic treasures increases daily. Both time and environmental hazards pose challenges to preservation, as do looters.

In Babylon, the restoration project includes refurbishing and reopening one of two museums on the site. Both were damaged in 2003 by coalition forces that used the historic site as a military base. The US State Department has provided $2 million in funding for the project, which will do more than preserve some of Iraq's history.[13] These funds will also be used to train Iraqis in skills that can be used in restoring other locations such as Ur, the capital of the Sumerian Empire. Training workers will improve their chances for employment, and preserving archaeological sites will help develop Iraq's tourism industry once traveling in the country is safe again.

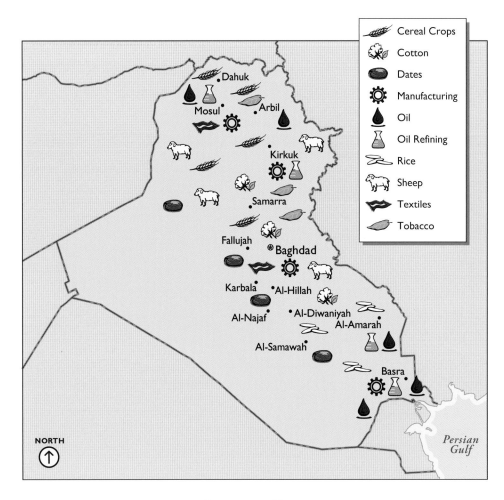

Resources of Iraq

of travel, such as camels and donkeys. The system of roads is more than 80 percent paved.[14]

Iraq also has a rail system, and some travel is done by boat. In addition, the country has an airline: Iraqi Airways. The nation's hub is Baghdad, and there are regional airports and military airfields as well.

WORKING TO INCREASE PROSPERITY

In addition to improving trade, tourism, and telecommunications, Iraq also has the daunting task of lifting its citizens out of poverty. The nation's unemployment rate is approximately 15 percent.[15]

According to the World Bank, Iraq was one of the most prosperous countries in the region in the early 1980s. But in 2005, after decades of Saddam Hussein's policies and ongoing war, approximately 10 percent of

IRAQ'S NEW CURRENCY

Under Saddam Hussein, inflation made the value of the Iraqi dinar fall dramatically. Other mismanagement meant that the currency was only issued in two denominations—250 and 10,000 dinars—which is similar to only having dimes and five-dollar bills to pay for everything. After the fall of Hussein in 2003, the US Treasury Department assisted the new provisional government in creating a new currency. The old dinars, which pictured Hussein, were destroyed and new ones were printed in six denominations. The new banknotes include figures and symbols from Iraqi history and culture.

the population lived on less than one US dollar per day.[16] Deteriorating infrastructure, including electric and sewer systems, contributes to the problem. Many Iraqi children are forced to work to support their families and thus have their education cut short, and many households have plunged into long-lasting poverty after the death of a principal breadwinner. In 2008, an estimated 25 percent of Iraqis lived below the poverty line.[17]

The situation is improving, however, as the country stabilizes. In 2010, the national GDP was $117.7 billion when adjusted for purchasing power, ranking Iraq sixty-fourth in the world. Also in 2010, the per capita GDP was $3,600, up from $3,500 in 2008.[18]

As the Iraqi people go about their lives, they are constantly met by the challenges caused by the conflicts that have plagued the nation for years, and their economic situation is no exception. Still, the Iraqis move forward. With time and continued support, the nation will hopefully become stronger and more secure. These improvements will benefit Iraq on multiple levels, from the quality of the people's lives to the general status of the nation.

A victim of Iraq's crumbling infrastructure, this girl fetching water must walk past an open sewage channel.

CHAPTER 9
IRAQ TODAY

Even with all the violence, destruction, and uncertainty Iraqis have experienced over the last several decades, they continue to go about their daily lives. Mothers shop at local markets, buying the ingredients they need to prepare the evening meal. Young women stop at clothing stores to admire the latest fashions by their favorite designers. Young men kick around soccer balls. Children play. Men chat over coffee.

For many Iraqis, family is the center of their lives. Iraqis cherish family, which includes immediate family members, extended family members, and members of their tribe, particularly in rural areas. During the war, the struggle for basic necessities disrupted family networks, as people focused on caring for their closest relatives and were unable to provide hospitality to more distant relatives. Lately, this situation has been improving.

Religion also plays a role in the daily lives of most Iraqis. In addition to requiring prayers five times throughout the day, Islam also dictates

A farming family from outside Baghdad

TEENAGE LIFE

Today's Iraqi teenagers grew up during a time of economic sanctions. In addition, they may have faced traumatic events as children, such as hunger, the fear of violence, or the death of a loved one. In general, the quality of life in Iraq decreased during these teens' lives, as electricity and drinkable water became more difficult to get and the education system deteriorated.

Many Iraqi teens must get jobs to contribute to their families' finances. Working teens have little time for leisure or entertainment.

Cultural changes have constrained teens' lives as well. In the past 20 years, the dress code for girls and women has become increasingly strict. Teen girls and boys are segregated for the most part.

Individuals react to difficult times in different ways. Some teens dream of leaving the country, getting an education, or having enough money to buy new clothes. Others become depressed over their life's circumstances or angry at the Iraqi government or Western nations. Some teens join terrorist organizations such as al-Qaeda. Across Iraq, most teens have to grow up quickly.

people's food choices and, for many, clothing choices. However, the Iraqi people have less strict dress requirements than their counterparts in other areas of the Middle East, including Saudi Arabia, stemming from years of secular Ba'thist rule. In fact, some Iraqis have adopted fashions common in the West. However, as religious groups gain power, women are increasingly pressured into dressing more conservatively.

EDUCATION

Education has suffered greatly since the 1990s, beginning with the Gulf War. Iraqi children are required to take part only in primary education, which

Children in a girls' school raise their hands.

is for students ages six to 12. Secondary education is available for children ages 12 to 18, but it is not required.

Education in Iraq saw tremendous growth in the 1960s, 1970s, and 1980s. During these decades, the government oversaw developments in education and funded schools at all levels. But during the 1990s, the economic sanctions placed on Iraq caused a major downturn in education, as many students left school to work and access to necessary resources such as textbooks declined. The wars of the 1990s took a toll on higher education as well, as many professors left the country and those who remained became isolated from international colleagues and research.

Arabic names and places often have multiple spellings in English.

Declining enrollment in Iraqi schools was reported by the United Nations Educational, Scientific, and Cultural Organization (UNESCO). In 2007, less than half of all Iraqi boys (42 percent) were enrolled, and even fewer girls (30 percent) were enrolled.[1] According to the United Nations Children's Fund (UNICEF), only 10 percent of Iraqis finish high school.[2]

Given this decline in education, Iraq's literacy rate dropped dramatically in the late 1990s and early 2000s. In 2007, UNESCO estimated the literacy rate at less than 60 percent for Iraqi adults. Iraqis in rural areas and women were estimated to have even lower rates. Only 37 percent of women in rural areas were thought to be literate.[3] More recently, literacy among Iraqi youth has improved. In 2010, UNICEF reported literacy rates among young Iraqis ages 15 to 24 with young men at 85 percent and young women at 80 percent.[4]

Education in Iraq continues to suffer because much of the nation's school infrastructure was lost in the war. To restore its system of education, the nation must rebuild or refurbish destroyed and dilapidated schools. In addition, it must provide textbooks and other necessary resources, especially well-trained teachers.

MOVING FORWARD

As the new Iraq continues moving forward, the government and its citizens must address multiple issues to create a secure

IRAQIGIRL: DIARY OF A TEENAGE GIRL IN IRAQ

In 2004, a 15-year-old Iraqi girl living in Mosul began a blog. In 2009, much of her blog was published in *IraqiGirl: Diary of a Teenage Girl in Iraq*. In the book, the girl's name is Hadiya, which was chosen to protect her true identity.

On October 7, 2004, Hadiya wrote about her problems returning to school:

> *Hello again. Bad news. School began last Saturday so we go to school every day now. The headmistress of our school gave me the oldest biology book. It was published in 1995. That means I was six years old when it was published! But the problem became worse.*

> *When I got home, Najma [her older sister]... took it from me because hers did not have all the pages.*

On October 25, Hadiya wrote about the severity of life in Iraq:

> *I had a physics examination.... But I don't care about the exams the way I did before. There are plenty of things that I think about now, plenty of problems that I can't fix.... Every day I say that life can't get worse, but I find that it can.... I am sure that none of you could live one day in Iraq. In Iraq now there is no happy word in our dictionary.[5]*

nation with a stable infrastructure, a healthy environment, and a strong economy. Each of these tasks will be challenging alone; together, they may be overwhelming. The Iraqi people will have to work together to build a more prosperous future.

Although Iraq's new government has proven stable, security in the country has not. At the beginning of 2011, the bombings, shootings, and murders that have been part of daily life for many years continued. As the number of US troops continues to decrease, securing the nation and making it a safe place to live may prove daunting.

Improving security in Iraq will help resolve many other key issues and strengthen the nation. For example, having increased security will help develop the tourism industry and foster economic growth, as people

DEATH TOLL IN IRAQ

The war in Iraq has resulted in the deaths of many people—many of them civilians. In fact, tens of thousands of Iraqi civilians have been killed, in addition to almost 5,000 members of coalition military troops.[6] The exact number of civilian deaths is not known and may never be, but documented civilian deaths from the violence in Iraq stood at approximately 100,000 in early 2011. And as the nation continued to struggle for stability and peace, the first week of April 2011 saw the loss of approximately three dozen lives in various locations across Iraq.[7]

Iraqis claim a generator, a valuable item in a country with unreliable electricity.

RECEIVING SUPPORT

Iraq's survival and initial recovery were supported by a variety of organizations, including other governments and national and international agencies. These groups provided assistance in a variety of areas, including health, housing, agriculture, and education.

However, support in Iraq has diminished. In September 2010, the *Environment News Service* reported that the number of nongovernmental organizations (NGOs) in Iraq has decreased dramatically, from 6,600 following the 2003 invasion to 500 in September 2010.[8]

Azzam Alwash, the founder and chief executive officer of Nature Iraq, noted the role of ongoing violence in the situation: "Funding has been steadily eroding over the past three years, with the increased violence in Iraq signaling to international donors that Iraq is not stable and that investment there may be lost."[9] In addition, Iraq's own NGOs are suffering because of limited funds and lack of support from the government.

from the Middle East, the West, and around the world will likely begin visiting Iraq. Expanding tourism may also help put aside misconceptions about Iraq and its people that have been created over the years by negative events and publicity.

Improved security will also likely foster growth in other areas of Iraq's economy. Over time, other nations and international companies will feel more confident about doing business with Iraq. An increase in business will require hiring more workers, helping to lower Iraq's unemployment rate, which is currently high.

An Iraqi police officer stands guard in Basra. Iraqis must improve security in order to rebuild their country.

And as more Iraqis obtain employment, they will be able to put money back into their economy.

To create a healthy, productive society, Iraq must help its people obtain life's necessities—especially water. Projects such as Nature Iraq are helping make that happen. This organization, along with Iraq's Ministry of Environment and other government agencies, is helping Iraqis in rural areas get safe drinking water. These organizations are also trying to restore Iraq's endangered marshlands.

Iraq undoubtedly has challenges to overcome as it moves ahead in the twenty-first century. And as the nation continues struggling with instability, violence, and personal security, several factors remain certain. Iraq has a long, revered history, dating back to the origins of civilization. Iraq also has a diverse people who value family, faith, culture, and tradition. Today, these people aspire to lead safe, healthy, productive lives. Taken together, these characteristics have made and will continue to make Iraq and its people an undeniable treasure.

Kurdish women voters display purple fingers, dyed when they cast their ballots. Iraqis are working together to build a better future.

TIMELINE

3500 BCE	The Sumerians settle in Mesopotamia.
1792–1750 BCE	Hammurabi rules Babylonia and creates the first written code of laws.
637 CE	Islam is introduced in Iraq.
1534–1918	The area that is now Iraq is part of the Ottoman Empire.
1918	The United Kingdom takes control of Iraq with a mandate from the League of Nations.
1921	The United Kingdom creates a monarchy in Iraq and names Faisal I its first king.
1932	Iraq becomes independent.
1958	Iraq's monarchy is ended by a coup.
1963	The Ba'th Party takes control of the government.
1979	Saddam Hussein becomes president of Iraq on July 16.
1980–1988	Iran and Iraq are at war.
1990	Iraq invades Kuwait on August 2, and the United Nations (UN) imposes sanctions against Iraq on August 6.

1991	Operation Desert Storm drives Iraqi troops out of Kuwait.
1996	Iraq accepts the UN's offer of a oil-for-food program and resumes selling oil in December.
1997	The oil-for-food program delivers its first shipment of food and medicine in March.
2003	The war in Iraq begins on March 20.
2003	Coalition forces take control of Baghdad on April 9.
2003	Hussein is captured on December 13.
2004	Iraq completes an interim constitution in March.
2005	Elections are held in Iraq on January 30.
2005	Iraqis vote to approve their new constitution on October 15.
2006	Hussein is executed on December 30.
2010	Jalal Talabani is reelected president in November.
2011	US forces are scheduled to pull out entirely by December.

FACTS AT YOUR FINGERTIPS

GEOGRAPHY

Official name: Republic of Iraq
(in Arabic, Jumhuriyat al-Iraq)

Area: 169,235 square miles
(438,317 sq km)

Climate: Predominantly hot and dry, with cooler temperatures and more moisture in the higher elevations of the north.

Highest elevation: Ghundah Zhur, 11,834 feet (3,607 m) above sea level (Note: Some sources claim existence of an unnamed peak reaching 11,847 feet [3,611 m] above sea level)

Lowest elevation: Persian Gulf, 0 feet (0 m) below sea level

Significant geographic features: Ghundah Zhur and Zagros Mountains, Tigris and Euphrates Rivers

PEOPLE

Population (July 2011 est.): 30,399,572

Most populous city: Baghdad

Ethnic groups: Arabs, 75 to 80 percent; Kurds, 15 to 20 percent; Turkmens, Assyrians, and others, 5 percent

Percentage of residents living in urban areas: 66 percent

Life expectancy: 70.55 years at birth (world rank: 145)

Language(s): Arabic (official), Kurdish (official in Kurdish regions), Turkic, Assyrian, Armenian

Religion(s): Islam, 97 percent (Shiite, 60 to 65 percent; Sunni, 32 to 37 percent); Christianity and other, 3 percent

GOVERNMENT AND ECONOMY

Government: parliamentary democracy

Capital: Baghdad

Date of adoption of current constitution: October 15, 2005

Head of state: president

Head of government: prime minister

Legislature: Council of Representatives; the constitution calls for creation of a second house, the Federation Council

Currency: Iraqi dinar

Industries and natural resources: Oil and chemicals

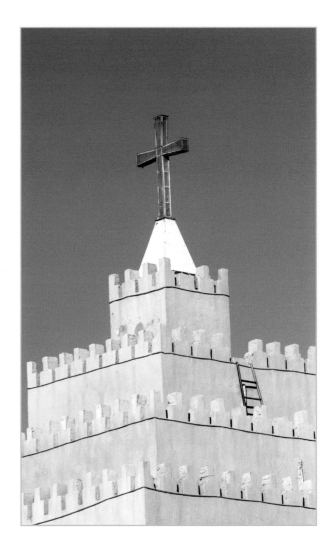

NATIONAL SYMBOLS

Holidays: The major secular holidays are New Year's Day and Army Day in January, Labor Day in May, Republic Day in July, and Ceasefire Day in August. The key Islamic holidays include Eid al-Fitr (Festival of Breaking Fast), Eid al-Adha (Festival of Sacrifice), and the Islamic New Year.

Flag: Three different-colored, equal-sized horizontal bands (red, white, and black), with the Takbir *Allahu akbar* (Arabic for "God is great") written in green across the white band

National anthem: "Mawtini" (My Homeland)

KEY PEOPLE

Hammurabi (ruled 1792–1750 BCE), Babylonian king known for his code of laws

Jalal Talabani (1933–), Kurdish politician who became president of Iraq in 2005

Saddam Hussein (1937–2006), twentieth-century dictator whose regime was toppled in 2003, executed in 2006 for mass murder

Nuri al-Maliki (1950–), prime minister of Iraq since 2006

GOVERNORATES OF IRAQ

Governorate; Capital

Al-Anbar; Al-Ramadi

Al-Najaf; Al-Najaf

Al-Qadisiyyah; Al-Diwaniyah

Al-Sulaymaniyyah; Al-Sulaymaniyyah

Arbil; Arbil

Babil, Al-Hillah

Baghdad; Baghdad

Basra; Basra

Dahuk; Dahuk

Dhi Qar; Al-Nasiriyyah

Diyala; Baqubah

Karbala; Karbala

Kirkuk; Kirkuk

Maysan; Al-Amarah

Muthanna; Al-Samawah

Ninawa; Mosul

Salah al-Din; Tikrit

Wasit; Al-Kut

GLOSSARY

bicameral

Having two chambers or houses.

caliphate

A state or empire ruled by the leader of Islam.

city-state

An independent region consisting of a city and the area surrounding it.

cuneiform

The oldest-known form of writing; developed by the Sumerians.

inflation

Continued increases in prices.

insurgency

Rebellion; revolution.

mandate

Order; authorize.

plateau

An area of land, usually large and flat, that is higher than the surrounding land.

republic

A government ruled by a chief of state, often a president, rather than a monarch.

salt flat

A now-dry desert lake, usually with a great amount of salt that glistens in the sun.

sectarian

Divided by sect or tribe.

steppe

A large area of land without trees.

topography

The shape of the land.

unicameral

Having one chamber or house.

ADDITIONAL RESOURCES

SELECTED BIBLIOGRAPHY

Ham, Anthony, James Bainbridge, César Soriano, Amelia Thomas, Jenny Walker, and Rafael Wlodarski. *Middle East*. 6th ed. London, UK: Lonely Planet, 2009. Print.

"Iraq." *Encyclopædia Britannica*. Encyclopædia Britannica, 2011. Web. 28 Jan. 2011.

United Nations Environment Programme. *Assessment of Environmental "Hot Spots" in Iraq*. Nairobi, Kenya: United Nations Environment Programme, 2005. Print.

"The World Factbook: Iraq." *Central Intelligence Agency*. Central Intelligence Agency, 16 Mar. 2011. Web. 23 Mar. 2011.

FURTHER READINGS

Fast, April. *Iraq: The Land*. New York: Crabtree, 2005. Print.

Fast, April. *Iraq: The People*. New York: Crabtree, 2005. Print.

Schaffer, David. *Iraq*. San Diego, CA: Greenhaven, 2003. Print.

Wrigley-Field, Elizabeth, ed. *IraqiGirl: Diary of a Teenage Girl in Iraq*. Chicago, IL: Haymarket, 2009. Print.

WEB LINKS

To learn more about Iraq, visit ABDO Publishing Company online at **www.abdopublishing.com**. Web sites about Iraq are featured on our Book Links page. These links are routinely monitored and updated to provide the most current information available.

PLACES TO VISIT

If you are ever in Iraq, consider checking out these important and interesting sites!

Al-Sulaymaniyyah's Grand Bazaar
Stretching for almost one mile (1.5 km) along Malawi Street, from the Sulaymaniyyah Palace Hotel to Ibrahim Pasha Street in Al-Sulaymaniyyah, the bazaar is open daily and offers the sites, sounds, and smells typical to Iraq.

Kurdish Textile Museum
This museum in Arbil showcases the beautiful handiwork of both settled and nomadic tribes.

National Museum of Iraq
This Baghdad museum is home to thousands of priceless artifacts of Iraq's long history.

SOURCE NOTES

CHAPTER 1. A VISIT TO IRAQ

1. "Climate of Iraq." *NOAA Satellite and Information Service*. US Department of Commerce, 26 May 2009. Web. 19 May 2011.

2. "The World Factbook: Iraq." *Central Intelligence Agency*. Central Intelligence Agency, 16 Mar. 2011. Web. 23 Mar. 2011.

3. US Department of State. "Travel Warning: US Department of State: Bureau of Consular Affairs." *Travel.State.Gov*. US Department of State, 12 Apr. 2011. Web. 19 May 2011.

CHAPTER 2. GEOGRAPHY: MORE THAN DESERT

1. "The World Factbook: Iraq." *Central Intelligence Agency*. Central Intelligence Agency, 16 Mar. 2011. Web. 23 Mar. 2011.

2. "Iraq." *Encyclopædia Britannica*. Encyclopædia Britannica, 2011. Web. 17 Jan. 2011.

3. Ibid.

4. "The World Factbook: Iraq." *Central Intelligence Agency*. Central Intelligence Agency, 16 Mar. 2011. Web. 23 Mar. 2011.

5. "Iraq." *Encyclopædia Britannica*. Encyclopædia Britannica, 2011. Web. 17 Jan. 2011.

6. "Shatt Al-'Arab." *Encyclopædia Britannica*. Encyclopædia Britannica, 2011. Web. 3 Feb. 2011.

7. "Iraq." *Encyclopædia Britannica*. Encyclopædia Britannica, 2011. Web. 17 Jan. 2011.

8. "Lake Hammār." *Encyclopædia Britannica*. Encyclopædia Britannica, 2011. Web. 3 Feb. 2011.

9. "Iraq." *Encyclopædia Britannica*. Encyclopædia Britannica, 2011. Web. 17 Jan. 2011.

10. Ibid.

11. Ibid.

12. Ibid.

13. "Country Guide: Iraq." *BBC: Weather*. BBC, n.d. Web. 14 Jan. 2011.

CHAPTER 3. ANIMALS AND NATURE: ADAPTED TO THE LAND

1. "Summary Statistics: Summaries by Country, Table 5, Threatened Species in Each Country." *IUCN Red List of Threatened Species*. International Union for Conservation of Nature and Natural Resources, 2010. Web. 18 Jan. 2011.

2. "Iraq Sulphur Fire Breaks Records." *BBC News*. BBC, 26 Oct. 2004. Web. 3 Feb. 2011.

3. "Iraq." *Encyclopædia Britannica*. Encyclopædia Britannica, 2011. Web. 17 Jan. 2011.

4. "Who We Are & What We Do." *NatureIraq.org*. Nature Iraq, n.d. Web. 30 Jan. 2011.

CHAPTER 4. HISTORY: NEW CIVILIZATIONS TO A NEW BEGINNING

1. Office of the Iraq Programme Oil-for-Food. "About the Programme." *UN.org*. N.p., 4 Nov. 2003. Web. 3 Apr. 2011.

2. JoAnne O'Bryant and Michael Waterhouse. "U.S. Forces in Iraq." N.p., 7 Apr. 2008. Web. 3 Apr. 2011.

CHAPTER 5. PEOPLE: VARIED AND DEVOTED

1. "The World Factbook: Iraq." *Central Intelligence Agency*. Central Intelligence Agency, 16 Mar. 2011. Web. 23 Mar. 2011.

2. Ibid.

3. Hussein D. Hassan. "Iraq: Tribal Structure, Social, and Political Activities." *FAS.org*. Library of Congress, 7 Apr. 2008. Web. 5 Apr. 2011.

4. "The People of the Kurdistan Region." *KRG.org*. Kurdistan Regional Government, 20 May 2010. Web. 3 Feb. 2011.

5. "The World Factbook: Iraq." *Central Intelligence Agency*. Central Intelligence Agency, 16 Mar. 2011. Web. 23 Mar. 2011.

6. "Iraq." *Encyclopædia Britannica*. Encyclopædia Britannica, 2011. Web. 17 Jan. 2011.

7. "The World Factbook: Iraq." *Central Intelligence Agency*. Central Intelligence Agency, 16 Mar. 2011. Web. 23 Mar. 2011.

8. Ibid.

9. Ibid.

10. Mitchell Bard. "The Jews of Iraq." *Jewish Virtual Library*. The American-Israeli Cooperative Enterprise, 2011. Web. 5 Apr. 2011.

11. Mitchell Bard. "The Jews of Iraq." *Jewish Virtual Library*. The American-Israeli Cooperative Enterprise, 2011. Web. 5 Apr. 2011.

CHAPTER 6. CULTURE: MIDDLE EAST MEETS WEST

1. "Basra's Pottery Industry Threatened with Extinction." *Iraqinews.com*. Iraqi News, 1 Jan. 2008. Web. 30 Jan. 2011.

CHAPTER 7. POLITICS: STARTING OVER

1. "Iraq's First Democratic Elections." *Mail Online*. Associated Newspapers, 25 Jan. 2005. Web. 7 Feb. 2011.

2. Ibid.

3. Ibrahim Touqan. "Iraq." *NationalAnthems.info*. NationalAnthems.info, n.d. Web. 30 Jan. 2011.

4. "Full Text of Iraqi Constitution." *MSNBC.com*. MSNBC.com, 16 Oct. 2005. Web. 20 May 2011.

5. "The World Factbook: Iraq." *Central Intelligence Agency*. Central Intelligence Agency, 16 Mar. 2011. Web. 23 Mar. 2011.

6. Associated Press. "Iraqis Defy Intimidation to Vote, Attacks Kill 36." *AZCentral.com*. AZCentral.com, 7 Mar. 2010. Web. 30 Jan. 2011.

7. Karen DeYoung. "Obama Sets Timetable for Iraq." *Washington Post*. Washington Post, 28 Feb. 2009. Web. 7 Feb. 2011.

8. Kevin Baron. "Gates to Warn Iraqis that Time is Running Out to Delay Withdrawal." *Stars and Stripes*. Stars and Stripes, 6 Apr. 2011. Web. 6 Apr. 2011.

CHAPTER 8. ECONOMICS: WORKING TOWARD RECOVERY

1. "The World Factbook: Iraq." *Central Intelligence Agency*. Central Intelligence Agency, 16 Mar. 2011. Web. 23 Mar. 2011.

2. Ibid.

3. "Iraq's Oil Exports Surge in January to Fresh Postwar Record." *Iraq Daily Times*. Iraq Daily Times, 2 Feb. 2011. Web. 3 Feb. 2011.

4. "The World Factbook: Iraq." *Central Intelligence Agency*. Central Intelligence Agency, 16 Mar. 2011. Web. 23 Mar. 2011.

5. Ibid.

6. "OPEC Share of World Crude Oil Reserves 2009." *OPEC.org*. Organization of the Petroleum Exporting Countries, 2011. Web. 30 Jan. 2011.

7. "The World Factbook: Iraq." *Central Intelligence Agency*. Central Intelligence Agency, 16 Mar. 2011. Web. 23 Mar. 2011.

8. "Countries: Iraq." *Revenue Watch Institute*. Revenue Watch Institute, 2011. Web. 20 May 2011.

9. "The World Factbook: Iraq." *Central Intelligence Agency*. Central Intelligence Agency, 16 Mar. 2011. Web. 23 Mar. 2011.

10. Barry Neild and Mohammed Tawfeeq. "Iraq Tourism Hangs in Balance at Babylon." *CNN.* CNN, 14 Jan. 2011. Web. 3 Feb. 2001.

11. "Iraq." *Encyclopædia Britannica.* Encyclopædia Britannica, 2011. Web. 17 Jan. 2011.

12. "The World Factbook: Iraq." *Central Intelligence Agency.* Central Intelligence Agency, 16 Mar. 2011. Web. 23 Mar. 2011.

13. "Iraq Tourism Hangs in Balance at Babylon." *CNN.* CNN, 14 Jan. 2011. Web. 3 Feb. 2001.

14. "Iraq." *Encyclopædia Britannica.* Encyclopædia Britannica, 2011. Web. 17 Jan. 2011.

15. "The World Factbook: Iraq." *Central Intelligence Agency.* Central Intelligence Agency, 16 Mar. 2011. Web. 23 Mar. 2011.

16. "Documents and Reports: Iraq—Strengthening Policy Making for Poverty Reduction, Employment Generation and Safety Net Development Project." *World Bank.* World Bank Group, 2011. Web. 20 May 2011.

17. "The World Factbook: Iraq." *Central Intelligence Agency.* Central Intelligence Agency, 16 Mar. 2011. Web. 23 Mar. 2011.

18. Ibid.

CHAPTER 9. IRAQ TODAY

1. "Assistance for Iraq: Education." *USAID for the American People.* US Aid, 9 Apr. 2007. Web. 7 Feb. 2011.

2. "Iraq: Background." *UNICEF.org.* UNICEF, 6 Apr. 2010. Web. 20 May 2011.

3. "Assistance for Iraq: Education." *USAID for the American People.* US Aid, 9 Apr. 2007. Web. 7 Feb. 2011.

4. "Iraq: Statistics." *UNICEF.org.* UNICEF, 2 Mar. 2010. Web. 7 Feb. 2011.

5. Elizabeth Wrigley-Field, ed. *IraqiGirl: Diary of a Teenage Girl in Iraq.* Chicago, IL: Haymarket, 2009. Print. 25.

6. "Operation Iraqi Freedom." *iCasualties.org.* iCasualties.org, 2009. Web. 3 Feb. 2011.

7. "Documented Civilian Deaths from Violence." *Iraq Body Count.* Iraq Body Count, 2011. Web. 3 Feb. 2011.

8. Samah Samad. "Iraq's Dwindling NGO Sector." *Environment News Service.* Environment News Service, 9 Sept. 2010. Web. 30 Jan. 2011.

9. Ibid.

INDEX

Kassites, 43
Koran, 64, 70, 83
Kurdish, 17, 62–64, 65, 80
Kurdish National Assembly, 90
Kurdistan, 42, 66, 77, 94, 96–98, 110
Kurds, 48, 51, 56, 61, 65–66, 68, 77, 84, 89, 90, 98, 99, 108
Kuwait, 19, 20, 22, 52–55, 106

language, 17, 62–66, 80, 94
leaders, current, 94–99
life expectancy, 61
literacy rate, 120
literature, 80
Lur, 66

Madan, 37, 66, 68
Madfai, Ilham Al, 80
Mala'ika, Nazik al-, 80
Maliki, Nuri al-, 95
marshlands, 15, 22–24, 32, 34, 36–39, 68, 127
Mesopotamia, 41, 42, 43–44, 72
mosque, 13, 70, 75, 85–86
Muhammad, 45, 46, 64, 70, 80
music, 44, 77–80
Mutlaq, Salih al-, 96

national anthem, 92
national capital, 10, 17
national museum, 10

national parks, 39
natural resources, 104–108
newspapers, 80

Obama, Barack, 99–100
official name, 17
oil, 48, 52, 54, 103, 104–108
Operation Desert Storm, 54
Organization of the Petroleum Exporting Countries, 106
Ottomans, 46–48

Persia, 44–46
Persian Gulf, 15, 20, 22, 54
plants, 32–37
political parties, 51, 98
population, 17, 61, 68, 72, 113
pottery, 42, 76
poverty, 80, 113–114
Presidency Council, 95–96
president, 17, 51, 52, 94–96, 98
prime minister, 50, 95–96, 98

Qasim, Abd al-Karim, 50–51

Rasheed, Oday, 81
regions, 20–25
religion, 17, 45, 65, 70–72, 75, 94, 117–118
religious sites, 70, 86, 94
Revolutionary Command Council, 52

Sabkhahs, 24, 37
Saffar, Amir, El, 79
salt flats, 24, 37
sandstorms, 10, 28
Sargon, 42
Shahristani, Husayn al-, 96
Shamma, Naseer, 80
Shatt al-Arab, 22
Shaways, Rowsch Nuri, 96
Shiite Muslims, 45, 51, 56, 66, 70–72, 84, 89, 93, 98, 99
Sinjar Mountains, 24
Sistani, Ali al-, 89
soccer, 81–83, 117
souk, 7–8
sports, 75, 81–83
Sumerians, 41, 42, 44, 76 80, 111
Sunni Muslims, 45, 70, 72, 84, 89, 93, 99
Syria, 19–20, 24, 46, 51, 64, 65, 84, 90, 107

Talabani, Jalal, 95, 98
tamarisk, 32–34
Taurus Mountains, 24
teenage life, 118, 121
Tigris River, 13, 22, 24–25, 34, 36, 41, 57, 65, 68
tourism, 110, 111, 113, 122–124
travel warning, 13
tribes, 48, 64–65, 72, 77, 99
Turkey, 19, 20, 25, 46, 65, 84, 107–108

INDEX CONTINUED

PHOTO CREDITS